Originally published with a slightly different cover in 2010, by Catersource llc, Minneapolis, Minnesota.

Reprint published by UBM Catersource llc
Minneapolis, Minnesota

1.877.932.3632
www.catersource.com

ISBN 978-0-9829918-0-0

Written by: Chef Eric LeVine

Photography by: Lou Manna and Chef Eric LeVine

Design and Art Direction: Jean Blackmer

Editorial Director: Linda Picone

Printed in the USA

Chef Eric and Catersource thank our sponsoring partners at TableCraft Products Company; EMI Yoshi, Inc.; BelGioioso Cheese, Inc.; Chef Rubber; and Pick on Us, Inc. for their support of this book and for the inspiring products they provided to make it happen.

stick it
SPOON IT
PUT IT IN A GLASS

By CHEF ERIC LeVINE

My editor, Linda Picone; art director, Jean Blackmer; and Jolene Ihle, who helped me shape this book. I appreciate the time and effort all of you put into making this book amazing.

Lou Manna and Joan O'Brien, who spent three crazy days shooting the pictures with me.

Pauline Hoogmoed, who, from the beginning of writing this cookbook, has been behind me and pushing me to make this book one of a kind! It was such a pleasure to work with you and the team.

Mike Roman, who years ago showed me how to stop playing checkers and start playing chess. Thank you, guru.

Pam Schindler, Sam Schindler, Robert Whalen, Matt Filipi, EMHS, Sun Tzu, Robert Greene, Sharon Annett, Gary Vaynerchuk. The direction and inspiration challenged me to change, think and explore. Thank you.

Mary Craft, Christine Emerson, Morgan Rose, Lajon Witherspoon, Clint Lowery, Vince Hornsby, John Connolly. The Colorado 2, Bridget Meyer and the Night Owl. Chef David Burke, Chef Cade & Ingrid Nagy, James Beard, Chef Domenic Chiaromonte, Carl Jones, Meryl and Andy Snow, Jean-louis La Massion, Lee Ho, Cathy and David Desroches. Jody Birnbaum, Pauline Parry, Chef Mike Purpura, Chef Joanne Purnell, Jack Milan, Chef Robert Szklayn, Mike "C.F," Jose, Anne Marie, Ann, Sandy, Amy, Danny, Maximo 1&2, Mike "Scooby-doo," Peter "the brick," Eddie Valentin, Villam, Estella, Mirta, O&A, little Jimmy Norton, Geddy, Neil and Alex. Everyone has a place here. You know why.

My kitchen staff over the past 30 years, who allowed me to excel and supported me every day. I am forever grateful to all of you! At the Marriott, Harvard Club, Pleiades, Lido Golf Club, EXQ Consulting, Chef Eric Catering and Events and everything in between.

My friends at the American Cancer Society, Leukemia & Lymphoma Society and Sloane-Kettering who have kept me going through all my battles.

Chef David Keener, I miss our talks of life and food!

All the partner sponsors of this book! Thank you for your time and dedication. Especially Amy, with TableCraft, who was there for me even while on her vacation.

Chef Eric LeVine

Fire it up!

Dedication

I would like to dedicate this book to my two amazing children, who have been the driving force behind everything I do. Stephanie and Ryan, my world is what it is because you two bring so much joy, insanity and laughter to my life. This book is also dedicated to Lorraine. Without your years of support, love and belief, I would never have become what I am. Through the good, bad and sometimes ugly, you have always been there. Always and forever.

To my family. Thank you for everything.

Mom, aka hippie. The world is a better place because of your heart; glad I can be there for you as you are there for me.

Dad and Jan, thank you for all the support over the years; I am glad to have you in my life.

Cathy, Joe, Peter, Bonnie, your positivity, support and unwavering love has been a blessing in so many ways.

Stan (big little brother, yes he is older), Jordana, Sasha, Andy, Ethan. Stacy, Ralph (Carols), Becky, Xenos (hello, hello), Laurie and Dr. Joe. All my nieces and nephews! I am so grateful to have each of you in my life. You are all crazy and amazing!

My grandmother Helen, who taught me from a young age that life should be lived to its fullest and love is unconditional. Your spirit lives every day; thanks for the lessons and know that now I understand.

My grandfather, who opened his home and his heart to teach me about so many things. No one will ever understand the impact you had on me.

FIRE IT UP!

Introduction

I'm happy with the hors d'oeuvre recipes I've put together in this book, and the process I used to create and test them, but there's more here than step-by-step instructions. If you follow the recipes exactly, you should come out with hors d'oeuvre that look just like the photos you see. I hope you also will use the recipes as a way to stimulate your own creativity. That's really the fun in being a chef, whether you're a professional or just preparing wonderful food for friends and family.

There's a kind of mathematical beauty to the 72 recipes in this book. I start with three key ingredients, then I show three different ways to use those key ingredients in hors d'oeuvre: skewered, served on a one-bite-sized spoon and in a mini-glass or cup. Each chapter has four different sets of key ingredients, so there are 12 recipes per chapter.

But the ways you can use the ingredients and the ideas don't stop there. Each recipe has suggested variations, sometimes substituting one key ingredient for a different flavor profile, sometimes using the same preparation techniques but with completely different ingredients. That means there are many more than 72 ideas presented—and that's not even including what you are inspired to do on your own.

I used "boxing" to come up with recipe ideas. "Boxing" is actually a way of getting outside the box when it comes to developing recipes—or any other effort that requires creativity. Here's a quick introduction to the boxing method:

- The first step in boxing is to forget about food. Clear your mind of ingredients and tastes for just a moment.

- Think about shapes instead. Using a pencil on a piece of paper, or on a paper plate, draw a circle, a square, maybe an octagon. It doesn't matter what the shape is. Draw three or four shapes.

- Now color the shapes. Combine colors that you have never thought about putting together. Remember, you're only thinking about shapes and colors, not food.

- As you look at each shape and color, begin to conceptualize food items. For instance if you have drawn a circle and filled it in with green, think about zucchini, or maybe a spinach ravioli.

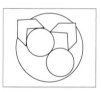

This process can be used to create appetizers, entrees, desserts and more. Creating from shapes and colors can open a new window of creativity for you.

Chef Eric LeVine | cheferic@exqconsulting.com

Fire it up!

SOME THINGS TO NOTE AS YOU USE THIS BOOK

Each recipe makes 10 to 20 hors d'oeuvre.
That's a relatively small number for a catered event,
but I've created them so they can be scaled up easily.

Some of the recipes use molecular gastronomy techniques.
These aren't as intimidating as the whole idea of molecular gastronomy once seemed,
but you may need equipment and ingredients that aren't part of your kitchen.
I've listed some of these items at the back of the book (page 214). In some cases, you can make
something similar without using special equipment or ingredients (a sauce instead of a foam, for example).
In others, you can do the same technique using equipment you already have
(a low-heat oven instead of a dehydrator). In still others, you can just skip that part of the recipe.

Temperatures listed are in Fahrenheit degrees.
Assume that ovens need to be preheated, unless there is a specific instruction not to.

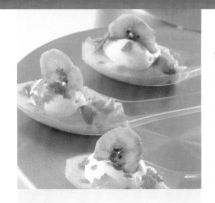

Seafood

TEMPTATIONS

**TUNA ◆ AVOCADO ◆ SOY
SMOKED SALMON ◆ SCALLION ◆ CAPERS
SHRIMP ◆ TOMATO ◆ CHILI
SCALLOPS ◆ CITRUS ◆ BASIL**

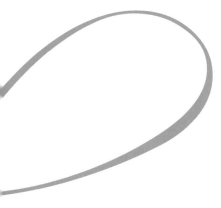

There's something almost immediately luxurious about seafood—although it is not necessarily expensive. The variety of flavors, textures and even appearance is great, from firm pink shrimp to melt-in-your-mouth whitefish. It's no wonder that many of our favorite hors d'oeuvre start with seafood.

This sampling focuses on some of the most popular seafood: tuna, salmon, shrimp and scallops. For most of the recipes, other fish and shellfish can be substituted for the main ingredient.

CHEF ERIC LEVINE

Seafood

TEMPTATIONS

TUNA ◆ AVOCADO ◆ SOY

SMOKED SALMON ◆ SCALLION ◆ CAPERS

SHRIMP ◆ TOMATO ◆ CHILI

SCALLOPS ◆ CITRUS ◆ BASIL

Stick

Spoon

Glass

Seared Tuna Loin with
Avocado and
Soy Gelées

Tuna Tartare with
Guacamole and
Soy Crisps

Tuna Carpaccio with
Avocado Mousse and
Soy Foam

14

16

18

SEAFOOD TEMPTATIONS

Makes about 10 servings

Seared Tuna Loin with Avocado and Soy Gelées

Ingredients/Seared Tuna Cube

1 lb tuna loin

1 oz Thai seasoning
(a combination that includes chili pepper, coriander, cumin, cinnamon, star anise and other spices)

1/2 oz sesame oil

Method/Seared Tuna Cube

Cut tuna loin into 3/4-inch cubes and dust with Thai seasoning.

Heat nonstick pan and add sesame oil. Once pan is hot, sear tuna quickly on each side for 1 minute, keeping the inside rare.

Ingredients/Avocado Gelée

1 fresh avocado

1/2 oz sour cream

1/4 oz lemon juice

1/2 tsp cilantro, chopped

1 tsp ground red pepper

1/2 fresh red pepper, seeded and diced fine

1/4 oz gelatin powder

2 oz warm water

Method/Avocado Gelée

Split avocado, remove seed and peel; put avocado meat in a bowl. Add sour cream and whisk until fully mixed. Add lemon juice and mix.

Add diced red pepper to avocado mixture, then add cilantro and ground red pepper.

Add gelatin to warm water and mix with whisk. Slowly fold gelatin and water into avocado mixture and place in a 4-inch square pan. Refrigerate and let set until firm, about 30 minutes.

Ingredients/Soy Gelée

6 oz soy sauce

1/4 oz gelatin powder

2 oz warm water

Method/Soy Gelée

Add gelatin to warm water and whisk until fully incorporated, then incorporate into soy sauce.

Pour into 4-inch square pan, refrigerate and let set until firm, about 30 minutes.

Assembly

Cut avocado and soy gelées into 3/4-inch cubes. Alternate soy gelée, avocado gelée and then seared tuna cubes on skewers.

Chef Notes
The tuna can be seared 1 hour before service, giving it time to cool so the exterior and interior are the same temperature.

Variations
Marinate a chicken breast in a soy-ginger-scallion marinade, then grill and cut into 1/2-inch pieces. Toss the cooked chicken with sesame seeds and chopped chives. You also can use hamachi, preparing it sushi-style. Marinate it lightly in a soy-ginger-scallion marinade.

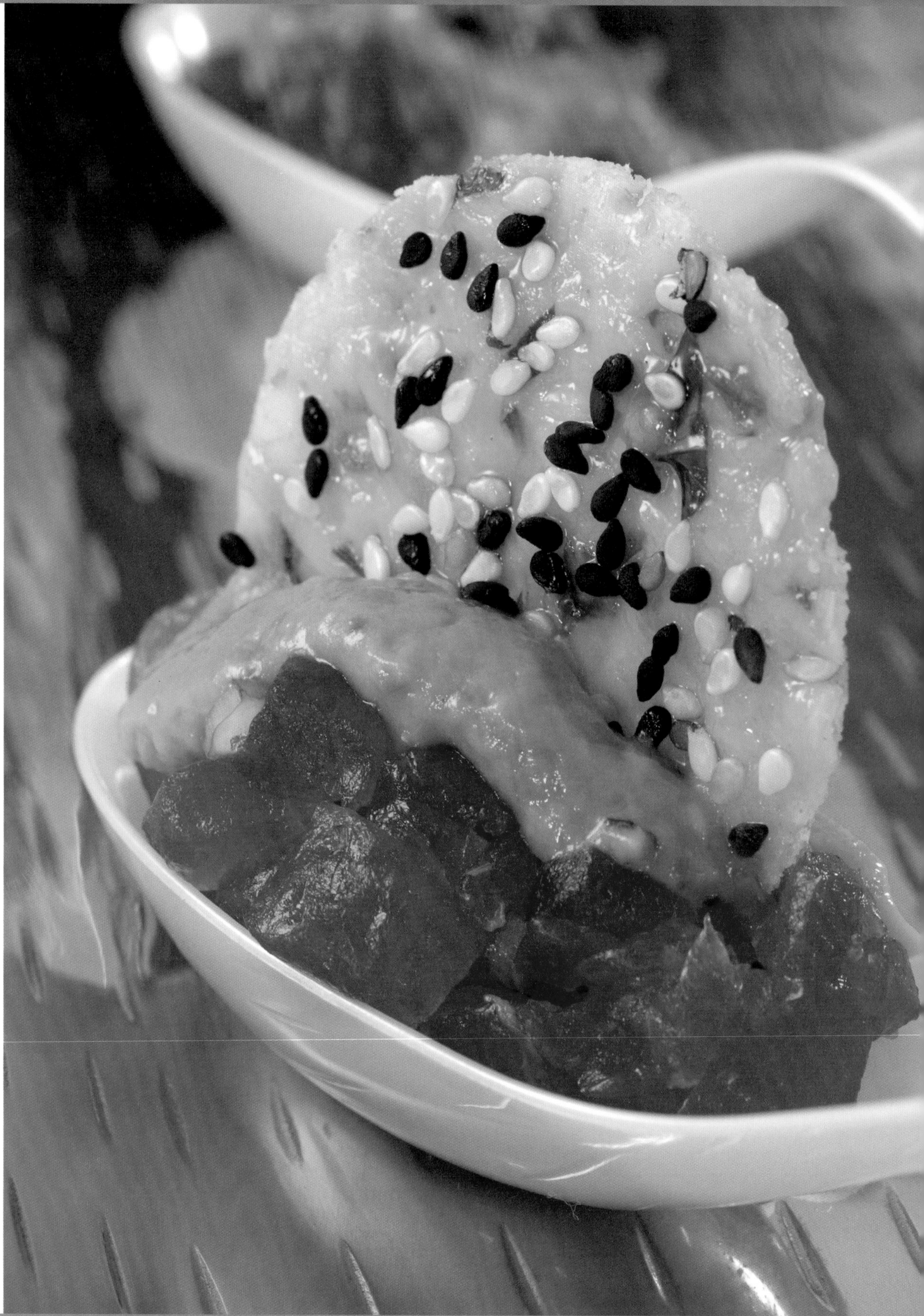

Makes about 10 servings

Tuna Tartare with Guacamole and Soy Crisps

IIngredients/Tuna Tartare

1 lb tuna loin

1 tsp sesame oil

1 tsp rice vinegar

1/4 tsp Asian red chili pepper flakes

Method/Tuna Tartar

Dice the tuna into 1/8-inch pieces and place in a mixing bowl. Combine sesame oil, vinegar and pepper flakes. Gently mix the oil and vinegar mixture into the tuna pieces, put in a hotel pan, cover with plastic wrap and store in refrigerator until ready for use.

Ingredients/Guacamole

2 ripe avocados

1/2 red onion, minced (about 1/2 cup)

1–2 Serrano chilies, stems and seeds removed, minced

2 Tbsp cilantro leaves, finely chopped

1 Tbsp fresh lime or lemon juice

1/2 tsp coarse salt

Dash of freshly grated black pepper

1/2 ripe tomato, seeds and pulp removed, chopped

Method/Guacamole

Cut avocados in half, remove seeds and scoop meat into a mixing bowl. Mash avocado with a fork. Add the minced onion, cilantro, lime or lemon, salt and pepper and mash some more. Start with half of one chili pepper and add to the guacamole to your desired degree of hotness. (Wash your hands thoroughly after handling chili peppers and keep your hands away from your eyes for several hours.)

Cover the mashed avocado mixture with plastic wrap. The wrap should be directly on the surface of the guacamole to keep air from reaching it. Refrigerate until ready to serve.

Just before serving, add the chopped tomato to the guacamole and mix.

Ingredients/Soy Crisps

1 cup flour

1/2 oz soy sauce

1 tsp sesame seeds

Method/Soy Crisps

Combine all ingredients in a bowl and mix well.

Spread mixture into 1-inch circles on a silicone mat.

Bake for 4 minutes at 350°, then cool to room temperature.

Assembly

Scoop tuna tartare into ceramic spoons and top each with guacamole. Place one soy crisp, standing up, into the guacamole in each spoon.

Chef Notes

If you make the soy crisps ahead of time, keep in an air-tight container so they don't become stale.

Work quickly with the avocado so it doesn't oxidize and change color while you're preparing the guacamole.

The guacamole recipe is flexible; start with the basic recipe and adjust ingredients to your taste.

Variations

For a more unusual option, cut a skate wing into small dice and marinate in a lime-tomato vinaigrette. Skate has a soft, scallop-like texture and goes well with guacamole. Sear just before assembly. You can also use a cilantro chicken salad instead of the tuna tartare.

Tuna Carpaccio with Avocado Mousse and Soy Foam

Ingredients/Tuna Carpaccio

1 lb Ahi tuna loin

1 oz sesame oil

1 oz rice wine vinegar

1/2 tsp Asian red chili pepper flakes

Method/Tuna Carpaccio

Slice the tuna into 10 1-oz slices.

Combine sesame oil, vinegar and pepper flakes. Use a brush to coat both sides of each piece of tuna with the sesame oil-vinegar mixture.

Put tuna pieces in a hotel pan, cover with plastic and store in refrigerator until ready to serve.

Ingredients/Avocado Mousse

1 ripe avocado

1/2 cup sour cream

1 tsp lemon juice

kosher salt and pepper to taste

Method/Avocado Mousse

Split the avocado and remove the seed. Scoop the pulp from the skin into a bowl, add sour cream and mix until it's fully incorporated. Fold in the lemon juice until it's fully incorporated, then add salt and pepper.

Put the mousse in a pastry bag and reserve in refrigerator until assembly.

Ingredients/Soy Foam

1/4 cup soy sauce

1/4 cup sour cream

1 tsp lecithin

Method

Puree soy sauce and sour cream in a blender or with a hand blender. Slowly add lecithin to the liquid and blend until bubbly. Reserve in pint container until service.

Assembly

Line a 3-1/2-oz cup with a 1-1/2-oz slice of tuna. Pipe avocado mousse in the middle of the tuna, then top with a teaspoon of soy foam. Garnish with black sesame seeds and radish sprouts. Serve with a mini fork.

Chef Notes

The tuna can be sliced ahead of time, but keep it covered with plastic wrap so it won't dry out.

When using fresh avocado, be sure to work quickly while mixing to avoid oxidation.

To spice up the tuna, sprinkle on a little Asian red chili pepper flakes

Variations

A mirin-seared salmon belly will give a nice buttery texture, that balances with the acidity of the Avocado Mousse.

Seafood

TEMPTATIONS

TUNA ◆ AVOCADO ◆ SOY

SMOKED SALMON ◆ SCALLION ◆ CAPERS

SHRIMP ◆ TOMATO ◆ CHILI

SCALLOPS ◆ CITRUS ◆ BASIL

Stick

Spoon

Glass

Smoked Salmon
Lollipops with
Bagel Dust

Smoked Salmon
Roulade with
Caper Relish and
Crispy Scallions

Smoked Salmon
Salad with Scallion
Caper Mousse

22

24

26

SEAFOOD TEMPTATIONS

Smoked Salmon Lollipops
with Bagel Dust

Ingredients/Smoked Salmon Lollipop

10 oz smoked salmon

8 oz cream cheese

2 Tbsp scallions, sliced thinly on the bias

1 tsp capers

2 tsp lemon juice

Method/Smoked Salmon Lollipop

Combine 6 oz smoked salmon, cream cheese, scallions, lemon juice and capers; mix in a stand mixer with a paddle until ingredients are combined. Place the mixture in the refrigerator until firm.

Remove mixture from refrigerator and roll into 10 balls. Place these on a sheet pan lined with parchment paper and put back in the refrigerator to firm, about 4 hours.

Cut the remaining 4 oz of smoked salmon into 10 1/4-inch julienne strips and reserve. Put a strip of smoked salmon around each of the cream cheese-smoked salmon balls.

Ingredients/Bagel Dust

1 plain bagel

salt and pepper to taste

Method/Bagel Dust

Slice the bagel into thin, paper-like pieces. Place the slices on a sheet pan lined with parchment paper and bake at 325° until dried, about 12 minutes. Remove from oven and let cool.

Once bagel slices are cool, pulse them in a food processer until they are in small, pebble-like chunks. Put the chunks in a bowl and season with salt and pepper.

Assembly

(Need 10 6-inch sticks for assembly.)

Push lollipop sticks into smoked salmon balls. Roll in bagel crumbs, using enough pressure to make sure that bagel "dust" sticks to the salmon balls.

Chef Notes
*The lollipop can be made 2-3 days ahead of time.
Be sure to cover in plastic to keep from getting dry.*

You can use seasoned breadcrumbs or crushed tortillas instead of the bagel dust for a different flavor profile.

Variations
You can make the cream cheese mixture with a homemade salsa and roll it with chopped fajita-style chicken for a Southwest flavor. Or, mix blue cheese into the cream cheese base, roll the lollipops in chopped crisped bacon and serve with a pipette filled with a port reduction.

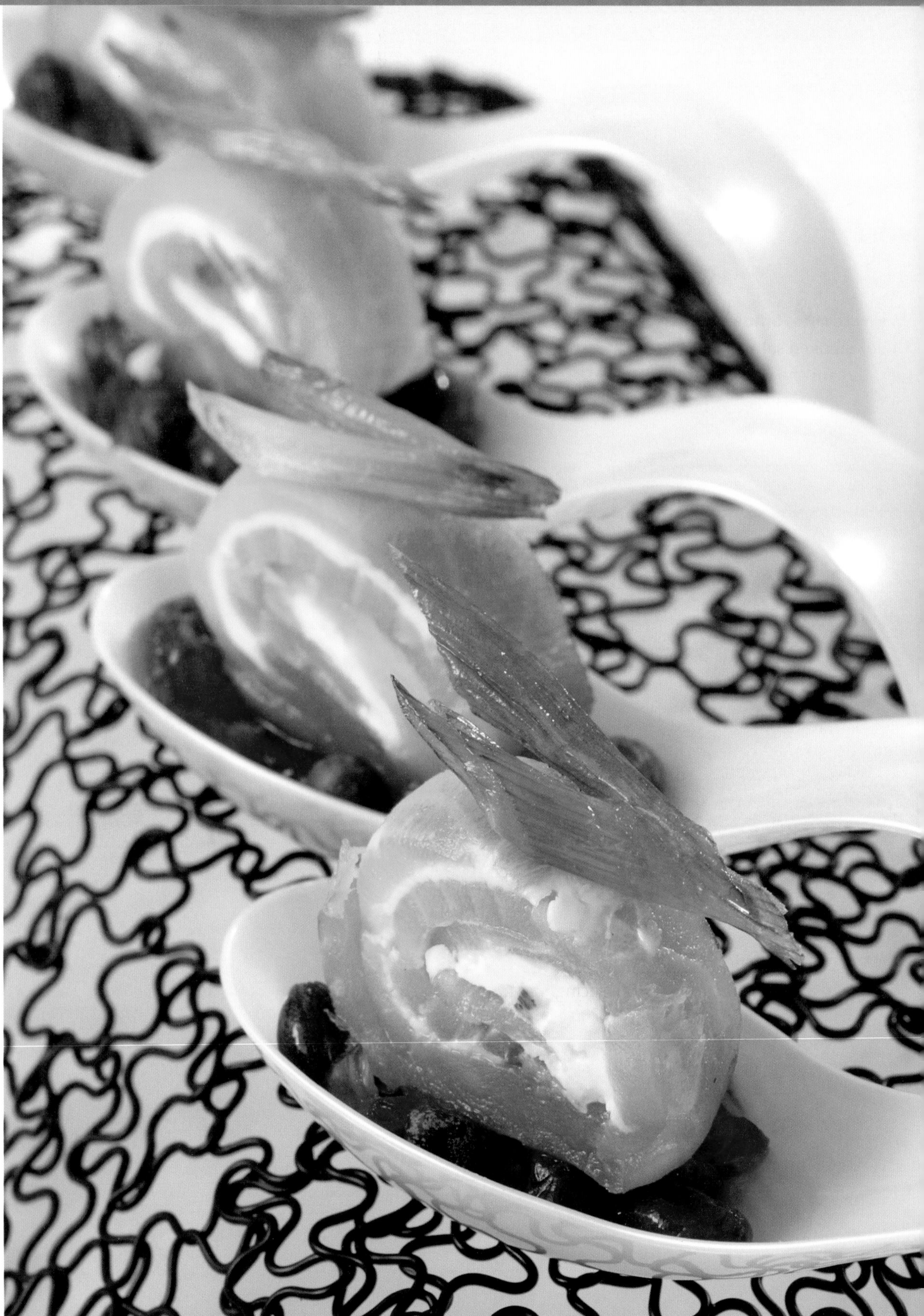

Smoked Salmon Roulade with Caper Relish and Crispy Scallions

Ingredients/Smoked Salmon Roulade

12 oz smoked salmon

4 oz cream cheese

1/4 cup chives

1 Tbsp lemon juice

1 oz capers

1/4 tsp maltodextrine

Method/Smoked Salmon Roulade

Cover a 12x12-inch work surface with plastic wrap. Slightly overlap pieces of salmon, laying them edge-to-edge to form one long rectangle.

Mix the cream cheese, chives, lemon juice and capers until soft and pliable.

With an offset spatula (a smaller spatula typically used for decorating and spreading), evenly spread the cream cheese mixture on smoked salmon. Leave ¼ inch on one side without cream cheese mix, so the roulade can be sealed.

Sprinkle maltodextrine on the exposed edges of the salmon. This will seal the edge and help the roulade keep its form when sliced.

Roll the smoked salmon lengthwise to create a roulade. Place the roulade at the edge of the plastic wrap and roll with the plastic on the outside. When it's rolled, twist the ends of the plastic wrap in opposite directions to force air out of the wrap.

Refrigerate for 2 hours to set before slicing.

Ingredients/Crispy Scallions

2 scallions

1/2 cup buttermilk

1/2 cup cornstarch

1 tsp black sesame seeds

Method/Crispy Scallions

Mix cornstarch and the black sesame seeds.

Cut the scallions, both green and white parts, into 1/2-inch pieces. Marinate the pieces in buttermilk for 5 minutes, then shake off excess buttermilk and dredge the scallion pieces in cornstarch mixture.

Fry until golden brown on the outside, about 6 minutes; reserve as garnish.

Ingredients/Caper Relish

1 tsp capers

2 tsp onions

4 tsp red wine vinegar

1 tsp honey

Method/Caper Relish

Combine all ingredients in a small saucepan. Cook over medium heat until mixture thickens.

Cool in a small bowl and reserve until ready to assemble.

Assembly

Remove plastic wrap from the roulade and slice into 20 rings.

Place caper relish into spoons. For each spoon, put one slice of the roulade on top of the caper relish and top with crisped scallions.

Chef Notes

This can be made without the maltodextrine, but may not look the same as the photo. Maltodextrine adds a nice shine to the smoked salmon.

You can make the roulade up to a week ahead of time and freeze. When ready to use, remove from the freezer 30 minutes before serving and allow to soften slightly before cutting.

Variations

Roulades can be made with many different ingredients. Marinate thin slices of tuna or hamachi and make a wasabi sesame mousse. Or use thin slices of cooked chicken instead of the salmon.

Smoked Salmon Salad with Scallion Caper Mousse

Ingredients/Smoked Salmon Salad

15 oz smoked salmon

2 tsp capers

3 tsp red onion, finely chopped

3 tsp cilantro, chopped

1 oz lemon juice

Method/Smoked Salmon Salad

Chop the smoked salmon and combine with onion and cilantro. Mix in the lemon juice and capers. Cover the bowl and refrigerate until ready to use.

Ingredients/Crepe Shell

1 cup all-purpose flour

2 eggs

3/4 cups milk

1/2 cup water

1/4 tsp salt

3 Tbsp butter, melted

Method/Crepe Shell

In a large mixing bowl, whisk together the flour and eggs. Gradually add in milk and water, stirring to combine. Add the salt and butter; beat until smooth.

Heat a lightly oiled griddle or frying pan over medium heat. Pour or scoop the batter onto the griddle, using about 1/4 cup for each crepe, to make a 4-inch circle. Tilt the pan with a circular motion so that the batter coats the surface evenly. The batter should make about 20 crepes.

Cook each crepe for about 2 minutes, until the bottom is light brown. Loosen with a spatula, turn and cook the other side. Remove and cool until assembly.

Ingredients/Scallion Mousse

2 scallions, chopped

5 oz cream cheese

1 oz capers

2 oz heavy cream

10 scallions (for assembly)

Method/Scallion Mousse

Combine cream cheese, heavy cream and capers in a mixer bowl. Using whip attachment, mix the ingredients at low speed, then turn it up to medium to whisk in air and create volume for the mousse. Mix until the mousse forms soft peaks. Just before turning off the mixer, add the scallions.

Assembly

Blanch 10 scallions for 20 seconds in boiling water, then shock in ice water. Remove from water and pat dry. Cut the root end off each scallion, then split the green part lengthwise to create 2 ribbons.

Place crepe shells on the work area, one at a time. Keep the remaining shells covered with a damp cloth to keep them from getting dry.

Place 1-1/2 oz of salmon salad in the center of each crepe.

Fold the sides of each crepe towards the center and pull up into a purse shape, then wrap with a piece of scallion and tie a knot.

Pipe Scallion Caper Mousse in the corners of the plate.

Chef Notes

Making fresh crepes is best, but you can save time without losing too much quality by using purchased crepes and cutting with a 4-inch cookie cutter.

Variations

Use a combination of smoked trout and smoked salmon. Pipe a little horseradish mousse in the bottom of the purse for a lively flavor.

Seafood

TEMPTATIONS

TUNA ◆ AVOCADO ◆ SOY
SMOKED SALMON ◆ SCALLION ◆ CAPERS
SHRIMP ◆ TOMATO ◆ CHILI
SCALLOPS ◆ CITRUS ◆ BASIL

Stick

Spoon

Glass

Shrimp Paper with
Poblano Chili Curry
Mist and Tomato Dust

Shrimp Roulade with
Tomato Compote and
Chili Mousse

Bloody Mary-Poached
Shrimp with Tomato
Onion Panna Cotta and
Chili Balsamic
Reduction

30

32

34

Chef Notes

Remember that this item is interactive. Explain to your guests that they mist the shrimp to get the full experience of the hors d'oeuvre. (Remind them to check which way the nozzle is pointed so they don't get mist in their eyes.) Encourage them to squeeze the lime on the shrimp for an extra pop of flavor.

Variations

Monkfish or swordfish, both of which have a substantial texture, can substitute for the shrimp. Either can be served with the Poblano Chili Mist, or you can make a Garlic Cilantro Mist, which has a more pungent flavor.

Shrimp Paper with Poblano Chili Curry Mist and Tomato Dust

Ingredients/Shrimp Paper

10 13/15 shrimp, peeled, deveined, tails off (save shells)

2 tsp olive oil

salt and pepper

curry powder

Tomato Dust (recipe below)

Method/Shrimp Paper

Butterfly shrimp by cutting back from tail to head. With a mallet, pound shrimp until it is about 1/8 inch thick.

Toss flattened shrimp in olive oil, season with salt, pepper, Tomato Dust and curry powder.

Grill on an open grill until lightly cooked, about 2–3 minutes on each side. Remove from grill and chill in refrigerator until ready to use.

Ingredients/Poblano Chili Mist

4 poblano chilies

1 tsp curry powder

2 Tbsp olive oil

salt and pepper

1/2 cup lime juice

1/4 cup shrimp stock (boil shells in water to make stock)

Method/Poblano Chili Mist

Split chilies in half and remove seeds. Toss with oil, salt and pepper.

Toss in oil , salt and pepper

Lightly grill on open grill until skin is charred, about 8 minutes.

Remove from grill and place in paper bag for about 20 minutes to allow chilies to steam. Remove chilies from bag and peel charred skin off.

Place chilies, curry powder, lime juice and shrimp stock in a blender and puree on high speed.

Strain through a fine chinoise to remove any impurities and lumps.

Pour into misting bottles and set aside until service.

Ingredients/Tomato Dust

6 vine-ripened tomatoes

kosher salt

Method/Tomato Dust

Cut each tomato into 6 wedges. Remove seeds and core. Sprinkle tomato wedges with salt.

Place in dehydrator for 12 hours. If you do not have a dehydrator, put on an open rack on a sheet pan and put in oven. Turn oven to 350° for 10 minutes (do not preheat oven). Turn heat off and leave tomatoes in for 15 hours.

Once tomatoes are dry, grind to powder in food processor or coffee grinder.

Reserve until preparing shrimp.

Ingredients/Grilled Lime

5 small fresh limes

2 tsp olive oil

salt and pepper

Method/Grilled Lime

Split limes in half on the bias; cut bottoms off straight. Toss limes in oil and season with salt and pepper.

Over an open flame, grill the limes with the flesh side down, so the centers will be lightly grilled, about 4 minutes.

Reserve for service.

Assembly

1/2 bunch chives, finely chopped

Weave shrimp on wooden skewers, leaving 1/2 inch near the sharp end of the skewer. Sprinkle chopped chives on both sides of the shrimp.

Stick the skewer into a lime half, so it's standing up.

Place skewers on a tray and serve with mist bottles.

Chef Notes

Be sure to keep your hands dry while working with transglutaminase. The transglutaminase links insoluble proteins together to form the "glue" in food. It is generally used to bind meats or proteins and is great for making sausages without using casings.

Transglutaminase can be used to form vegetable or even meat "noodles."

Variations

Scallops, lobster or salmon can be used instead of shrimp, for a somewhat upscaled option. You can also pound chicken breast thin, then sprinkle with tomato dust and roll.

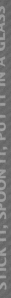

Shrimp Roulade with Tomato Compote and Chili Mousse

Ingredients/Tomato Dust
8 plum tomatoes
1 qt sundried tomato purée
1 cup fresh basil, chopped

Method/Tomato Dust
(Make Tomato Dust 2 days before you plan on making the roulade.)

Combine all ingredients in a food processor and purée until smooth, then drain using a China cap or fine strainer.

Place the mixture into a dehydrator or spread on a nonstick pan for at least 12 hours to dry.

Once the purée is dry, pass it through a tamis, cheese cloth or fine strainer to remove any clumps.

Reserve.

Ingredients/Shrimp Roulade
24 U15 Shrimp
4 tsp transglutaminase, divided
1 tsp kosher salt
1 tsp Tomato Dust
1/2 bunch cilantro

Method/Shrimp Roulade
Peel and devein the shrimp, then butterfly.

Lightly poach the shrimp in water, stock or lemon juice until flesh is just cooked, about 5 minutes. Remove from the liquid, then chill.

Lay butterflied shrimp side-by-side on a work surface covered with plastic wrap and sprinkle with 2 tsp transglutaminase.

Cover the shrimp with a second piece of plastic wrap and pound to create a "sheet" of shrimp. Remove the top piece of plastic wrap and heavily sprinkle the shrimp with Tomato Dust, then sprinkle with the other 2 tsp of transglutaminase.

Roll the "sheet" of shrimp, using the bottom piece of plastic wrap, to create a roulade. Twist the ends of the plastic wrap in opposite directions to squeeze out air.

Chill the roulade in the refrigerator until ready to serve.

Fry cilantro until crispy, then drain on paper towels, sprinkle with kosher salt and set aside.

Ingredients/Tomato Compote
2 small (5x6 size) tomatoes
1/2 cup chopped red onion
1/2 cup fresh basil
1/2 cup Balsamic vinegar
1/4 cup chopped garlic
1 tsp red pepper flakes
1 tsp sugar
2 tsp olive oil

Method/Tomato Compote
Dice tomatoes into 1/4-inch pieces.

Add olive oil to a hot 4-qt saucepan. Add the red onion and garlic and cook until translucent. Add the diced tomatoes and cook over medium heat until soft, about 10 minutes. Add remaining ingredients and bring to a simmer. Lower the heat and cook until the mixture is the consistency of paste, about 15 minutes, then remove from the heat, cool and set aside.

Ingredients/Chili Mousse
4 oz cream cheese
1/2 cup heavy cream
1/4 tsp each, kosher salt and white pepper
1/4 tsp chili powder
1/2 tsp chopped cilantro

Method/Chili Mousse
Combine all ingredients with a mixer, using whisk attachment. Then whisk on medium speed until the mixture is smooth and forms peaks, about 8 minutes.

Assembly
Slice the shrimp roulade into 1/4-inch rings.

Place tomato compote in spoons, almost covering spoon bottoms. Put one slice of roulade in each spoon, standing up.

Put Chili Mousse into a piping bag with a small star tip. Pipe onto the roulade on each spoon.

Sprinkle Chili Mousse with Tomato Dust. Top with fried micro-cilantro.

Chef Notes
*Don't use too much agar-agar when making the panna cotta.
While mixing the agar-agar into the liquid, test a small
amount for proper thickness (it should not be "hard" texture,
but both creamy and firm) and seasoning.*

Variations
*The panna cotta adapts to any number of flavors: garlic-basil,
jalapeño-cilantro or ginger-scallion-mirin and more. Shrimp
can work with any of these flavored panna cotta, but poach
them in lightly seasoned water, rather than the Bloody Mary
poaching liquid, so flavors won't conflict.*

SEAFOOD TEMPTATIONS

Bloody Mary-Poached Shrimp with Tomato Onion Panna Cotta and Chili Balsamic Reduction

Ingredients/Marinated Shrimp

20 U15 shrimp

20 wood skewers

6 cups tomato juice

2 tsp hot sauce

2 tsp Worcestershire sauce

1 tsp prepared horseradish

1 tsp celery salt

Method/Marinated Shrimp

Peel and devein shrimp, leaving tails on. Skewer the shrimp from the tail towards the head.

Combine the remaining ingredients in a saucepan and mix with a whisk. Place skewered shrimp into the saucepan, with the shrimp heads down in the liquid. Cook the shrimp over medium heat until tender, about 8 minutes. Watch carefully; shrimp cook quickly and you don't want the skewer end to get burned.

Ingredients/Tomato Onion Panna Cotta

1 oz sundried tomatoes

peanut or vegetable oil for oiling ramekins

2 Tbsp butter

2 cloves garlic, minced

1/2 cup red onion, minced

2 tsp tamari

2 Tbsp agar-agar flakes

2 cups crème fraîche

1 cup freshly grated Parmigiano-Reggiano

freshly ground black pepper to taste

salt to taste

1-1/2 Tbsp chopped chives

Method/Tomato Onion Panna Cotta

Place sundried tomatoes in a medium bowl and pour 1-1/2 cups boiling water over them. Leave until the tomatoes are completely softened, about 30 minutes. Lift the tomatoes out of the soaking water, reserving the water; rinse tomatoes in a sieve to remove any grit, then squeeze dry and mince. Line the sieve with several layers of paper towels and strain the soaking water through it into a small saucepan. Set aside.

Melt butter in a sauté pan over medium heat. Add the garlic and onion and sauté briefly, then add minced sundried tomato. Cook, stirring often, about 5 minutes. Stir in tamari, then transfer to a mixing bowl.

Add agar-agar flakes to the reserved sundried tomato water and mix well; let stand 10 minutes. Bring the water and flakes to a boil, stirring constantly, then reduce heat and simmer 10 minutes. Strain the water and agar-agar mixture through a sieve into the sundried tomato mixture, mixing well. Add crème fraîche and Parmigiano-Reggiano and mix well. Season with salt and pepper to taste. Fold chopped chives into cheese mixture.

Ladle 2 oz of the mixture into oiled 4-oz cups and let stand until set, about 1 hour in refrigerator.

Ingredients/Chili Balsamic Reduction

2 tsp chili powder

3 cups Balsamic vinegar

1/2 cup sugar

3 tsp cornstarch

3 tsp water

Method/Chili Balsamic Reduction

Combine chili powder, Balsamic vinegar and sugar in a saucepan. Bring the mixture to a simmer and cook until reduced by half, about 12 minutes.

Combine the cornstarch and water to make a slurry. While vinegar mixture is simmering, slowly add the cornstarch and water until the liquid is smooth and viscous. Remove from the heat and cool.

Assembly

Remove the panna cotta from the cups in which they set and place into service cups. Place Balsamic Reduction in pipette and place into the panna cotta in each service cup. Place one shrimp skewer into each cup, head down, and garnish with microgreens and celery.

Seafood

TEMPTATIONS

TUNA ◆ AVOCADO ◆ SOY

SMOKED SALMON ◆ SCALLION ◆ CAPERS

SHRIMP ◆ TOMATO ◆ CHILI

SCALLOPS ◆ CITRUS ◆ BASIL

Stick

Spoon

Glass

Seared Scallops
with Citrus Confit and
Fried Snow Pea Sprouts

Scallop Ceviche with
Citrus Compote and
Basil Foam

Basil Crusted Scallops
with Citrus Aioli and
Citrus Dust

38

40

42

Scallops, Citrus, Basil

Makes about 10 servings

Seared Scallops with Citrus Confit and Fried Snow Pea Sprouts

Ingredients/Citrus Confit

5 lemons

5 oranges

2 cloves garlic

2 tsp black peppercorns

6 sprigs fresh thyme

1 dried chili

1 bay leaf

1 cup salt

3 cups sugar

3 cups olive oil

Method/Citrus Confit

Cut the lemons and oranges in half and place in a stainless steel pan. Add all remaining ingredients except olive oil, cover with cold water and bring to a boil over medium heat. Reduce heat to maintain a slow simmer; too much heat will cause the lemons and oranges to fall apart.

Simmer for 15 minutes, then pour the contents of the pan, including liquid, into sanitized Mason jars. Seal and let cool in refrigerator for at least 8 hours.

When ready to use, scrape out the pith (the white layer between the peel and the flesh) of the lemons and oranges with a knife and cut pith into 1/2-inch strips.

Ingredients/Seared Scallops

30 10/20 dry (not frozen) scallops

1 tsp finely chopped garlic

1 tbsp finely chopped fresh basil

1 tsp finely chopped cilantro

1 oz lemon juice

1 oz orange juice

1 oz lime juice

1 tsp chili powder

Method/Seared Scallops

Remove any connecting muscles from the side of each scallop.

Mix all other ingredients to create a marinade.

Alternate two strips of citrus confit and 3 scallops on each skewer, starting and ending with a scallop. Dredge each skewer in marinade and let rest 1 hour in the refrigerator before service.

Ingredients/Fried Snow Pea Sprouts

4 snow pea sprouts

1 cup olive oil

kosher salt to taste

Method/Fried Snow Pea Sprouts

Heat oil to 350°. Drop snow pea sprouts into oil and fry until crisp, then remove from oil and drain on paper towels.

Before service, lightly crumble the sprouts into crispy flakes.

Assembly

Heat a nonstick pan over medium heat. Sear one side of each skewer for 3 minutes, then flip and sear the opposite side for 2 minutes, or until scallops are cooked through. Remove scallops from the pan and sprinkle snow pea sprouts on both sides.

Chef Notes

The citrus confit can be made up to 5 days ahead and held in the refrigerator for later use.

Use dry, or fresh, scallops for the best results. IQF scallops have a higher water content and may become soft and break apart during preparation.

For best quality, fry the snow pea sprouts just before service.

Variations

Sea bass can be substituted for the scallops; its texture works well with the crust.

Scallop Ceviche with Citrus Compote and Basil Foam

Ingredients/Scallop Ceviche

8 Tbsp tomato juice

8 Tbsp fresh orange juice

8 Tbsp fresh lemon juice

8 Tbsp fresh lime juice

1/2 bunch cilantro, stemmed and chopped

2 red onions, peeled and diced

8 Tbsp ketchup

2 jalapeño chilies, split, seeded and finely chopped

1 tsp hot red pepper sauce

salt and fresh ground black pepper to taste

10 10/20 scallops

Method/Scallop Ceviche

In a bowl, combine all ingredients except the scallops. Remove the connecting tissue from the side of each scallop and split scallops in half lengthwise, then place them in the bowl of marinade and marinate for 12 hours in the refrigerator.

Ingredients/Citrus Compote

1 orange

1 lemon

1 lime

1 red onion, peeled and finely diced

1/4 bunch fresh cilantro, finely chopped

1/4 bunch fresh mint, finely chopped

1/2 tsp red pepper flakes

Method/Citrus Compote

Peel and section the lemon, lime and orange. Cut the sections into 1/4-inch pieces and combine with other ingredients and mix well. Set aside.

Ingredients/Basil Foam

1/2 cup heavy cream

1/4 cup vegetable stock

1 bunch fresh basil

kosher salt and pepper

Method/Basil Foam

Combine all ingredients in a 1-qt container and puree with a hand blender. Slowly lift the blender to the surface and agitate until a foam forms.

Assembly

Place a half scallop on each spoon. Layer with 1/4 tsp Citrus Compote, then place another scallop on the compote. Layer another 1/4 tsp Citrus Compote, then top with Basil Foam and a micro basil leaf.

Chef Notes

Using 1 gm of lecithin or agar-agar to make the foam will keep it stable and bubbly for a longer period of time. You can use cream as a base, but for off-premise events, lecithin works best. If you are using cream, reduce the amount if using both agar-agar and/or lecithin. Both products can be purchased through Chefrubber.com

Variations

Salmon, hamachi, or snapper can be used instead of scallops. Use horn melon or pomegranate with a touch of mint to create a different flavor profile.

Makes about 10 servings

Basil Crusted Scallops with Citrus Aioli and Citrus Dust

Ingredients/Basil Crusted Scallops

10 10/20 scallops in dry pack

1 bunch fresh basil

1 cup panko bread crumbs

2 garlic cloves

kosher salt

white pepper

1 tsp olive oil

1 Tbsp amaranth leaf pieces

Method/Basil Crusted Scallops

Remove the connecting muscle from the side of each scallop.

Lightly chop the basil with oil in a food processor. Add the garlic, then slowly add panko bread crumbs to create basil crumbs. Salt and pepper to taste.

Toss the scallops in the crumb mixture and lightly press crumbs onto each scallop so it's well coated.

Place the scallops on a sheet pan lined with parchment paper and bake at 350° for 12 minutes or until scallops are cooked through and tender. Hold no longer than 5 minutes before service.

Ingredients/Citrus Aioli

1/2 tsp saffron threads

1/4 cup hot water

2 garlic cloves

2 egg yolks

1 cup blanched slivered almonds

kosher salt

1/2 orange, juiced

3 cups extra-virgin olive oil

water as needed to thin

Method/Citrus Aioli

Steep the saffron in hot water for 3 minutes; remove using a small strainer.

Put saffron, garlic, egg yolks, almonds, salt and orange juice into a blender and blend. Drizzle in the olive oil until the mixture is emulsified. Set aside.

Ingredients/Citrus Dust

1 lemon

1 lime

1 orange

kosher salt and white pepper to taste

Method/Citrus Dust

Remove the rinds from the citrus and dry them in a dehydrator. If you don't have a dehydrator, put the rinds on a sheet pan and keep in a 125° oven for 20 minutes, then turn the oven off and allow the rinds to dry in the closed oven for 8 hours, until they are dry and brittle.

Put the dried citrus rinds, kosher salt and white pepper in a food processor and pulse until it turns to powder. Pass the powder through a fine China cap or sieve to get a fine texture. Set aside.

Assembly

Put a scallop in the bottom of each cup. Top with Citrus Dust, then pipe a small dollop of Citrus Aioli on top and finish with a popcorn shoot. Garnish with amaranth leaf pieces.

Chef Notes

You can use mayonnaise as the base for the aioli to save time. Use a cup of mayonnaise, add saffron prepared the way the recipe shows and finish with a touch of citrus such as orange, lemon and lime.

Instead of making the Citrus Dust from scratch, you can purchase a flavored dust from a number of online companies.

Instead of popcorn shoots, you can use beet micro greens for their red color

Variations

The crust on this works well with many kinds of fish. Try orange roughy or halibut.

Poultry SENSATIONS

CHICKEN ◆ TOMATO ◆ CELERY
DUCK ◆ FIGS ◆ ONION
TURKEY ◆ CRANBERRIES ◆ SAGE
PHEASANT ◆ APPLE ◆ PORK

Poultry is a basic for good reasons: It takes on flavors beautifully but, when cooked correctly, has its own lovely taste. In general, chicken holds well and so can be prepared in advance and taken to an event without losing flavor or texture. It works with almost any ingredient and can be prepared successfully in many different ways.

Here you have chicken and turkey recipes, as you'd expect, but also the surprise of duck and pheasant.

Poultry
SENSATIONS

CHICKEN ◆ TOMATO ◆ CELERY

DUCK ◆ FIGS ◆ ONION

TURKEY ◆ CRANBERRIES ◆ SAGE

PHEASANT ◆ APPLE ◆ PORK

Stick

Spoon

Glass

Oven Roasted Curried
Chicken with Pickled
Celery and Garlic
Goat Cheese
Stuffed Tomatoes

48

Torn Chicken with
Spicy Tabasco
Tomato Confit and
Celery Chips

50

Bloody Mary
Tomato-Poached
Chicken with
Celeriac Mousse

52

Oven Roasted Curried Chicken with Pickled Celery and Garlic Goat Cheese Stuffed Tomatoes

Ingredients/Oven Roasted Curried Chicken

10 jumbo chicken tenders

2 tsp curry powder

2 tsp olive oil

1/4 tsp red pepper flakes

salt and black pepper

Method/Oven Roasted Curried Chicken

Pound chicken tenders lightly until they are about 1/4 inch thick.

Toss in oil and season with curry powder, salt, black pepper and red pepper flakes. Marinate overnight in refrigerator.

Ingredients/Pickled Celery

2 celery stalks, remove leaves and roots

1 cup red wine vinegar

1 cup sugar

1 tsp black peppercorns

1 tsp cinnamon

1 tsp whole star anise

Method/Pickled Celery

On mandoline set to make about 1/4-inch slices, slice celery lengthwise to create long thin strips.

Combine all ingredients except celery in a saucepan over medium heat and bring to a boil. Turn off heat and let cool to 70°. Add celery and refrigerate overnight.

Reserve for skewering

Ingredients/Garlic and Goat Cheese Stuffed Tomatoes

30 small cherry tomatoes

15 oz goat cheese

2 tsp garlic, chopped and roasted

2 tsp coriander

2 tsp chopped chives

1 tsp red onion, diced, sautéed and cooled

salt and pepper

Method/Garlic and Goat Cheese Stuffed Tomatoes

Using a small knife, cut a small hole in the top of each cherry tomato.

Combine all other ingredients in a bowl and mix with a spoon until smooth. Place into a piping bag with a small pastry tip.

Pipe 1/2 oz goat cheese mixture into each cherry tomato.

Reserve for skewering.

Assembly

Weave 1 piece of chicken and 1 strip of celery around 3 cherry tomatoes on each skewer (see photo).

Heat oven to 350°. Place skewers on a sheet pan and bake for 15–18 minutes, until chicken is cooked all the way through. Remove from oven and serve.

Chef Notes

Be sure that you pound the chicken to 1/4-inch thickness or less, otherwise the tomatoes and celery will be overcooked before the chicken has fully cooked.

Variations

Pork or flank steak can be used instead of the chicken. Marinate pounded slices of pork tenderloin in soy, ginger and scallions. Instead of tomatoes, use marinated cremini mushrooms; instead of pickled celery, use marinated or pickled zucchini ribbons.

Makes about 10 servings

Torn Chicken with Spicy Tabasco Tomato Confit and Celery Chips

Ingredients/Torn Chicken

1 lb boneless, skinless chicken breasts

2 cups tomato juice

1 cup chicken stock

2 stalks celery, roughly chopped

1/2 medium red onion, chopped

1 tsp red pepper flakes

Method/Torn Chicken

Clean any excess fat from chicken breasts.

Pour the tomato juice and chicken stock into a pot and add half the chopped celery and onions. Place the chicken breasts into the pot, then cover with the remaining celery and onion, plus the pepper flakes. Cook over a medium flame for 20 minutes or until the chicken can be shredded with a fork.

Remove the chicken from the pot and shred while still hot, then set aside to cool.

Ingredients/Spicy Tabasco Tomato Confit

12 pear tomatoes

1 red onion, diced

2 tsp Tabasco sauce

1/4 bunch cilantro, chopped

1/4 cup tomato juice

2 tsp honey

1 tsp red pepper flakes

2 tsp olive oil

Method/Spicy Tabasco Tomato Confit

Heat the oil in a pan and cook the onions until clear and translucent, about 6 minutes.

Remove seeds from pear tomatoes and dice into 1/4-inch pieces. Add onions and cilantro to tomatoes, then add tomato juice, honey, Tabasco sauce and pepper flakes. Simmer over low flame for 15–20 minutes until mixture is reduced, then remove from flame and cool. The confit should be thick and pliable.

Ingredients/Celery Crisps

2 celery stalks

kosher salt

Method/Celery Crisps

Slice the celery into 1/8-inch slices and sprinkle with salt.

Dry in a dehydrator for 7-10 hours until crisp.

Assembly

Put enough torn chicken in each spoon to make one bite. Top the chicken with a 1/2 tsp of Tomato Confit and then sprinkle with 2 pieces of dried celery just before service.

Chef Notes

If you don't have a dehydrator, put the celery slices on a sheet pan and keep in a 125° oven for 20 minutes, then turn the oven off and keep them in the closed oven for 8 hours, until they are crisp.

Variations

Braised beef brisket or slow-roasted pork loin can be substituted for the chicken. To change the flavor profile completely—and to upscale the item, use butter-poached shrimp, scallop or lobster.

Makes about 20 servings

Bloody Mary Tomato-Poached Chicken with Celeriac Mousse

Ingredients/Bloody Mary-Poached Chicken

2 lbs boneless, skinless chicken breasts

3 cups Bloody Mary mix

1 cup chicken stock

1 red onion, roughly chopped

1 jalapeño, roughly chopped

1 tsp olive oil

kosher salt

white pepper

Method/Bloody Mary-Poached Chicken

Clean any fat off chicken breasts and dice into 1/4-inch pieces. Season with salt and pepper.

Sauté onion and jalapeño pieces in oil until soft, about 6 minutes. Add chicken pieces and sauté until lightly browned, about 5 minutes. Add the liquids and bring temperature to 160°. Cook over medium flame for 20 minutes, until chicken pieces are cooked through.

Remove chicken pieces from pot and let cool.

Ingredients/Celeriac Mousse

4 oz celeriac root

1 tsp prepared horseradish

1/2 cup sour cream

1/4 bunch chervil, finely chopped
(reserve the rest of the bunch for garnish)

1/4 cup heavy cream

kosher salt

white pepper

Method/Celeriac Mousse

Peel the celeriac root and then grate into a mixing bowl. Add the horseradish and sour cream to the celeriac. Then add the heavy cream and whisk briskly. Season with salt and pepper. Fold the finely chopped chervil into the mousse.

Assembly

Place 2 oz of poached chicken cubes into the bottom of each glass.

Put the Celeriac Mousse into a piping bag with a circle tip and then pipe on top of the chicken in each glass.

Garnish with chervil or micro-greens.

Chef Notes

Both the chicken and the mousse can be made ahead of time and assembled just before service.

Place some chiffonade of celery leaf on top of the chicken before the celery mousse for a lighter flavor.

Variations

Instead of chicken, try a lemon-rubbed pork with chili for a spicier, very different flavor.

Poultry
SENSATIONS

CHICKEN ◆ TOMATO ◆ CELERY

DUCK ◆ FIGS ◆ ONION

TURKEY ◆ CRANBERRIES ◆ SAGE

PHEASANT ◆ APPLE ◆ PORK

Crispy Duck with
Pickled Onions and
Grilled Figs

Oven-Roasted Duck,
Fresh Fig Purée and
Grilled Shallots

Poached Duck with
Caramelized Figs and
Onion Marmalade

56

58

60

Crispy Duck with Pickled Onions and Grilled Figs

Ingredients/Crispy Duck

1 Muscovy duck breast

2 tsp olive oil

2 garlic cloves, finely chopped

1 sprig fresh thyme, chopped

kosher salt

white pepper

Method/Crispy Duck

Using a paring knife, score the duck breast through the skin.

Combine the oil and spices and rub into the duck.

In a hot pan, sear the skin side of the duck breast until it's golden brown, about 6 minutes.

Bake the duck breast at 325° for 20 minutes, or until its internal temperature is 145°, then remove from oven and set aside to cool.

Ingredients/Pickled Onions

20 red pearl onions

2 cups orange juice

1 cup sugar

1/2 cup red wine vinegar

Method/Pickled Onions

Combine all ingredients in a pot, bring to a simmer on the stove and then turn heat off. Let the mixture steep for 1 hour, then cool and refrigerate until ready to use.

Ingredients/Grilled Figs

10 Mission figs

2 tsp olive oil

kosher salt

white pepper

Method/Grilled Figs

Quarter figs into wedges. Toss the wedges in the olive oil and season with salt and pepper.

Heat a grill and lightly grill the figs on both flesh sides. Cool and set aside.

Assembly

Slice the duck breast into 20 thin slices; fold each slice in half to skewer. Put the duck, onions and figs on 10 skewers in this order: one folded piece of duck breast, one piece of pickled onion, one fig, a second piece of duck breast, a second piece of pickled onion, a second piece of fig.

Chef Notes
Be very careful not to overcook the figs; if cooked too long, they will be too soft to skewer easily.

Variations
To add a refreshing zip to this item, pickle the figs in a sugar-vinegar solution. It will not only change the fig flavor, it will add another dimension to the duck as well.

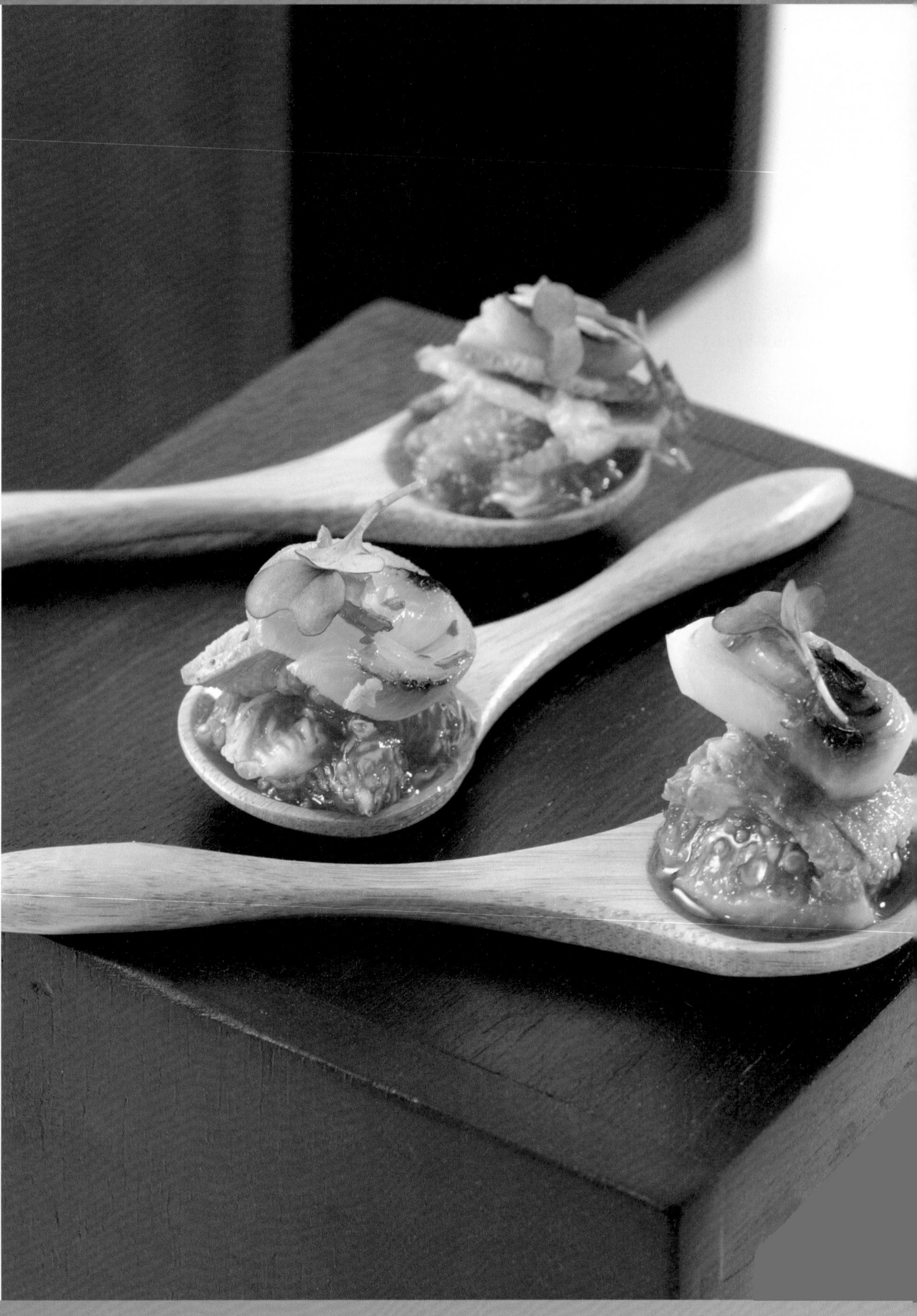

Makes about 20 servings

Oven-Roasted Duck, Fresh Fig Purée and Grilled Shallots

Ingredients/Oven Roasted Duck

1 Muscovy duck breast

1 tsp olive oil

kosher salt

white pepper

Method/Oven Roasted Duck

Score the skin on the duck breast in a diamond pattern; season with salt and pepper.

Heat oil in a pan over high heat. Put the scored duck breast into the pan, skin side down, then reduce the heat to medium. As fat from the breast melts into the pan, use it to baste the top of the breast. Once the skin is crisp, turn the duck breast over and sear the other side.

Once it's been seared on both sides, the duck breast should be placed in a 325° oven for 12 minutes.

Remove the breast from the oven and let cool.

Remove the skin from the duck breast, finely dice and reserve. Slice the breast into 40 paper-thin slices and set aside.

Ingredients/Fresh Fig Puree

6 black Mission figs

1 tsp honey

2 tsp Balsamic vinegar

1/4 bunch fresh lavender

kosher salt

Method/Fresh Fig Puree

Trim the stems from the figs. Pull the lavender leaves off the stems.

Combine all ingredients in a blender and puree until smooth. Set aside.

Ingredients/Grilled Shallots

4 shallots, thinly sliced

1 tsp olive oil

kosher salt

ground white pepper

Method/Grilled Shallots

Toss shallot slices in olive oil and season with salt and pepper.

Put foil on top of a grill until it gets hot. Put the shallot slices on the foil and grill them until they are slightly charred, about 6 minutes, then take them off and let them cool. Set the shallots aside for later use.

Assembly

Put 1/2 tsp of Fig Purée in each spoon, then top with two thin slices of duck breast. Put Grilled Shallots on top of the duck breast, then sprinkle on a little crisped duck skin.

Chef Notes

If fresh lavender is not available, use a pinch of dried lavender, but be careful: If you use too much dried lavender, the flavor in the puree will be too strong.

Variations

Squab or pheasant can be substituted for the duck—great for fall menus. Use leeks or cipollini onions instead of shallots for a different take on the onion flavor.

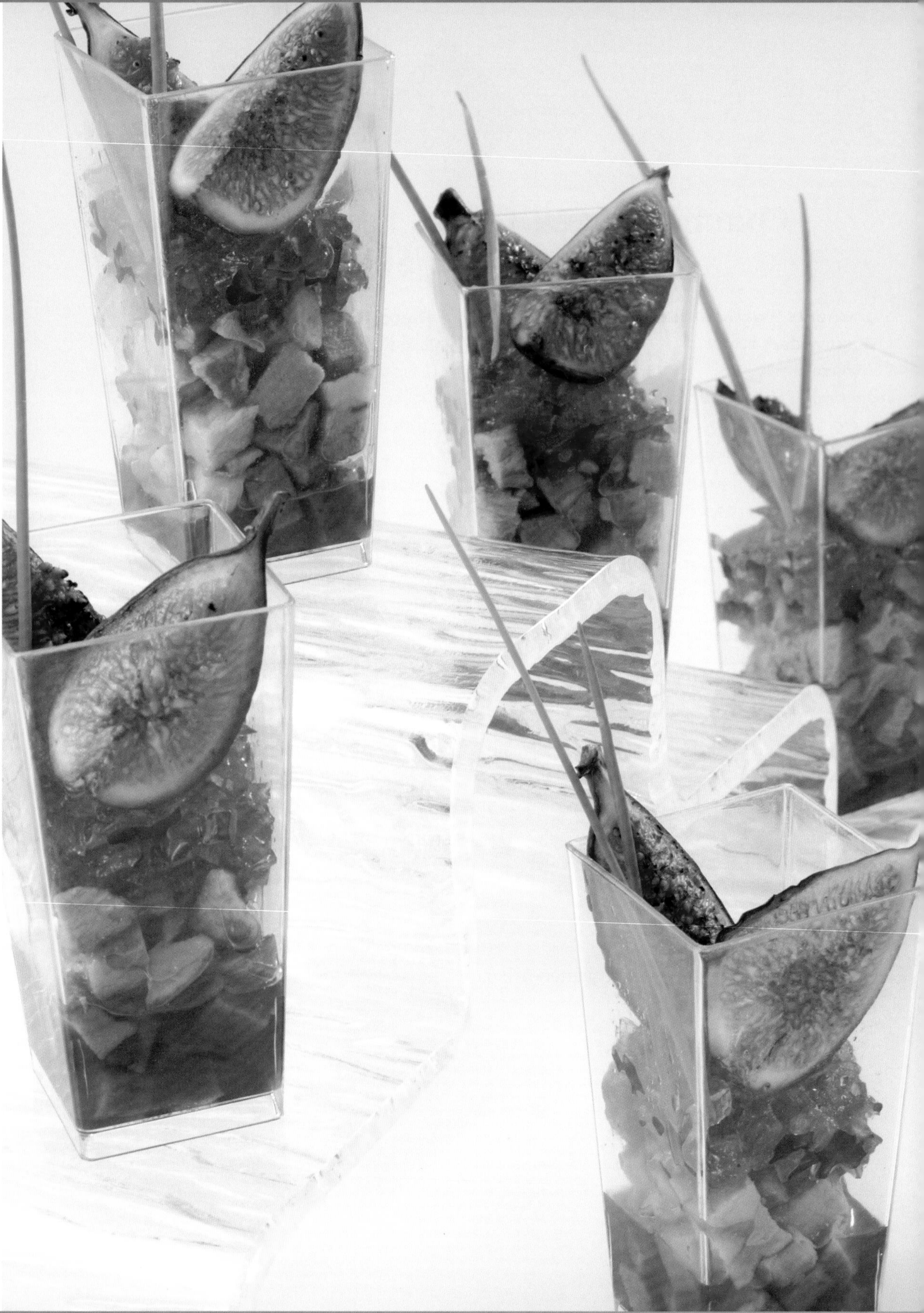

Poached Duck with Caramelized Figs and Onion Marmalade

Ingredients/Poached Duck

1 Muscovy duck breast

2 cups cranberry juice

1 cup duck or chicken stock

2 sprigs rosemary, roughly chopped

3 garlic cloves, smashed

Method/Poached Duck

Remove the skin from the duck breast.

Combine the liquids in a pan and add rosemary and garlic. Put duck breast into the liquid.

Cook over medium heat until the liquid gets to 145°, then lower the heat and poach for about 20 minutes, until the duck breast has an internal temperature of 145°.

Remove the duck breast from the liquid and let cool, then dice into 1/4-inch pieces and set aside.

Ingredients/Caramelized Fig

5 black Mission figs

2 tsp honey

1/4 tsp fresh ginger, finely grated

1 sprig of rosemary, finely chopped

Method

Remove the stems from the figs and quarter each into wedges.

Toss all ingredients together in a bowl and place on a sheet pan; roast in a 325° oven for 11 minutes, until the figs become tender and caramel-colored.

Set aside to cool.

Ingredients/Onion Marmalade

2 red onions, cut in 1/4-inch dice

3 tsp honey

1 tsp red pepper flakes

Method/Onion Marmalade

Combine all ingredients in a saucepan; cook over medium heat for about 15 minutes, until the onion pieces are tender.

Remove from heat, cool and set aside.

Assembly

Put duck pieces in the bottom of 10 service cups or glasses. Place 1/2 tsp of Onion Marmalade on top of the duck in each cup, then add 2 fig pieces.

Chef Notes

Simmer, do not boil, the duck breast or it will become tough. Poaching should be kept a temperature of no higher than 145°.

Variations

Chicken, turkey, pheasant or even pork can be used instead of duck breast. Black garlic will give the duck an earthier flavor, which is nice for the fall and winter. It also changes the appearance of the dish, as well as the flavor.

Poultry
SENSATIONS

CHICKEN ◆ TOMATO ◆ CELERY

DUCK ◆ FIGS ◆ ONION

TURKEY ◆ CRANBERRIES ◆ SAGE

PHEASANT ◆ APPLE ◆ PORK

Stick

Spoon

Glass

Grilled Turkey
Mini-Burgers with
Cranberry Muffins and
Sage Aioli

64

Turkey Dumplings with
Cranberry Glaze and
Sage Dust

66

Shaved Pepper Turkey
with Cranberry Stuffing
and Sage Apple
Chutney

68

Turkey, Cranberries, Sage

Chef Notes

The turkey burger needs to be cooked fresh on-site and served immediately.

Warm the muffin before serving to give it the best flavor.

Variations

This concept can be transformed in many ways, such as:

Scallion Ginger Muffin with Thai Chicken Salad

Fire House Onion Muffin with BBQ Beef Brisket

Jalapeño Muffin with Salsa Marinated Shrimp and Cilantro Aioli

Makes about 20 servings

Grilled Turkey Mini-Burgers with Cranberry Muffins and Sage Aioli

Ingredients/Grilled Turkey Mini Burgers

1 lb ground turkey

1 cup honey mustard and onion pretzels, crushed

1/4 cup finely chopped green bell pepper

1 egg, beaten

salt and pepper to taste

Method/Grilled Turkey Mini Burgers

Mix the ground turkey, crushed pretzels, green bell pepper and egg in a bowl; season with salt and pepper. Form into 20 patties and place on a sheet pan.

Grill patties on a hot grill for about 3 minutes on one side and 2 minutes on the other, until turkey is cooked—but not dry—with an internal temperature of 150°.

Ingredients/Cranberry Muffins

3/4 cup plus 2 Tbsp and 1 tsp all-purpose flour

1/4 cup plus 3 Tbsp white sugar

3/4 tsp baking powder

1/4 tsp baking soda

1 tsp orange zest

3/4 tsp ground nutmeg

1/2 tsp ground cinnamon

1/4 tsp ground ginger

3 Tbsp plus 1-3/4 tsp shortening

1/3 cup orange juice

1/2 tsp vanilla extract

7-8 eggs (depending on size), beaten

2/3 cup chopped cranberries

3/4 cup plus 3 Tbsp and 2 tsp chopped walnuts

Method

Mix together the flour, sugar, baking powder, baking soda, orange zest, nutmeg, cinnamon and ginger. Cut in the shortening, then stir in juice, vanilla, eggs, cranberries and nuts. Pour the batter into a 20-mini-muffin tin that has been sprayed or greased with oil and bake at 350° for 25 minutes or until brown.

Set aside.

Ingredients/Sage Aioli

1 egg yolk

1 tsp Dijon mustard

1/2 bunch fresh sage, chopped

1 cup extra-virgin olive oil

1/2 clove garlic, minced

lemon juice to taste

salt and pepper to taste

Method/Sage Aioli

Whisk together the Dijon mustard and egg yolk in a bowl. Slowly pour in the olive oil, while whisking rapidly.

After all the olive oil is incorporated, blend in the garlic and lemon juice. Season with salt and pepper. Add the sage and mix thoroughly.

Assembly

Split each mini-muffin horizontally.

Spoon 1/4 tsp Sage Aioli on each muffin bottom. Put a Mini Burger on top of the aioli, then top the burger with another 1/4 tsp aioli. Add the top half of the Cranberry Muffin and skewer with a pick.

Chef Notes
Leftovers can be frozen in an airtight container for up to 2 months.

The Sage Dust can be made up to 2 days ahead of the time and stored in a cool dry place.

Variations
Instead of baking in the oven, poaching the dumplings in cranberry, mint and juniper stock will give the dumplings a deep rich flavor.

Turkey Dumplings with Cranberry Glaze and Sage Dust

Ingredients/Turkey Dumplings

(for dumplings)

1–3/4 cups all-purpose flour

1/2 tsp baking powder

1/4 tsp baking soda

1/2 tsp salt

1/4 cup butter

1/4 cup chopped fresh herbs, such as chives and parsley

3/4 cup buttermilk

1 large egg

(for turkey mixture)

1/4 cup butter

1/2 cup all-purpose flour

3 cups turkey stock

1 tsp chopped fresh thyme

1 bay leaf

salt and pepper to taste

1/4 tsp Worcestershire sauce

4 cups diced cooked turkey

2–1/2 cups mixed vegetables: zucchini, squash, peas, carrots

Method/Turkey Dumplings

Whisk together the 1-3/4 cups flour, baking soda, baking powder and salt. Cut in 1/4 cup butter until the mixture resembles coarse breadcrumbs. Stir in the chopped herbs.

Cover the dough and refrigerate until ready to use.

Melt 1/4 cup butter in a 3-qt saucepan over medium heat. Whisk in 1/2 cup flour and cook for 1 minute.

Add turkey stock to the pan, 1/2 cup at a time, mixing in to prevent lumps. When all the stock has been added, season with the thyme, bay leaf, salt, pepper and Worcestershire sauce. Simmer for 15 minutes, then stir in the turkey and vegetables and bring to a simmer again.

Once the mixture is simmering, transfer it to a 4-qt baking dish with a lid.

Whisk the buttermilk and egg together and then add to the reserved dumpling mixture. Stir together until flour is evenly moistened.

Scoop tablespoons of the batter on top of the turkey mixture, leaving space between the dumplings (they will almost double in size as they cook).

Put the lid on the baking dish and bake at 350° for 25–30 minutes.

Ingredients/Cranberry Glaze

12 oz fresh cranberries

1 cup granulated sugar

1/4 bunch fresh sage

1 cup chicken stock

Method/Cranberry Glaze

Combine all ingredients in a saucepan. Bring to a boil and simmer for 30 minutes.

Purée the mixture with a hand blender, then cook for 5 more minutes.

Ingredients/Sage Dust

1 bunch sage

2 oz maltodextrine

1/2 oz olive oil

kosher salt

Method/Sage Dust

Toss the sage leaves in salt, then dry in a dehydrator for 8 hours.

Once the sage leaves are dry, put them in a blender and grind to a powder.

Add olive oil to the sage powder in the blender, then add maltodextrine to create volume.

Taste for intensity of flavor; add salt if needed to make the sage flavor stronger.

Assembly

Spoon 1/4 oz Cranberry Glaze into each spoon. Place 1–2 Turkey Dumplings on top of the glaze. Sprinkle a little Sage Dust on top of the Turkey Dumplings.

Shaved Pepper Turkey with Cranberry Stuffing and Sage Apple Chutney

Ingredients/Shaved Pepper Turkey

1-1/2 lbs turkey breast

2 tsp olive oil

1/2 bunch sage, chopped

2 cups apple juice

1 cup turkey stock

20 whole sage leaves

kosher salt

white pepper

Method/Shaved Pepper Turkey

Rub the turkey breast with oil, salt, pepper and chopped sage.

Place turkey on rack into roasting pan; pour apple juice and turkey stock into bottom of pan.

Cover pan with foil. Bake turkey breast in 350° oven for 40 minutes, or until internal temperature is 155°.

When breast is cooked, remove from pan, cool and set aside.

Fry 20 sage leaves until crisp.

Ingredients/Cranberry Stuffing

1/2 cup butter

3/4 cup chopped celery

1 onion, chopped

4 cups oatmeal bread cubes, dried in the oven

1/2 cup dried cranberries

1/2 tsp dried sage leaves

1/2 tsp dried thyme leaves

1 tsp salt

1/4 tsp pepper

1/4 to 1/3 cup chicken stock

Method/Cranberry Stuffing

In a large skillet, melt 1/2 cup butter and cook celery and onion until tender, about 6-8 minutes.

In a large bowl, combine the remaining ingredients, except the stock. Pour the celery mixture over the ingredients in bowl and toss gently with two spoons. Add the chicken stock and toss mixture until bread cubes are lightly moistened. Cool and set aside.

Ingredients/Sage Apple Chutney

6 Granny Smith apples, peeled, cored and diced into 1/4-inch cubes

2 cups fresh or frozen cranberries

1 cinnamon stick

1 bay leaf

1 Tbsp pickling spice

1 Tbsp black mustard seeds

2 Tbsp sugar

1-inch piece of ginger

1 cup apple juice

1/2 cup apple cider vinegar

Method/Sage Apple Chutney

Put ingredients in a saucepan and simmer for 10–15 minutes until the apples are tender. Remove the chutney from the heat, cool and set aside.

Assembly

Slice the turkey as thin as possible into 20 pieces.

Place 2 tsp stuffing into each cup. Top with 1 oz shaved turkey, then 1 tsp Apple Chutney. Garnish with a fried sage leaf.

Chef Notes
You can serve this warm or at room temperature.
This item is a great holiday pick-and-go hors d'oeuvre.
The preparation is simple and fast so there is no fuss.

Variations
Instead of the stuffing, make cranberry-sage
mini-biscuits and serve the turkey on top of the biscuits.

CHICKEN ◆ TOMATO ◆ CELERY

DUCK ◆ FIGS ◆ ONION

TURKEY ◆ CRANBERRIES ◆ SAGE

PHEASANT ◆ APPLE ◆ PORK

CHEF ERIC LeVINE

Stick

Spoon

Glass

Roasted Pheasant with
Roasted Apple and
Pancetta Roulade

Grilled Pheasant with
Apple Chutney and
Prosciutto Crisps

Poached Pheasant with
Apple Mousse and
Crispy Pork Belly

72

74

76

POULTRY SENSATIONS

Makes about 20 servings

Roasted Pheasant with Roasted Apple and Pancetta Roulade

Ingredients/Roasted Pheasant

2 pieces pheasant breast

2 tsp olive oil

2 sprigs fresh thyme, finely chopped

2 springs fresh sage, finely chopped

2 shallots, finely chopped

kosher salt

ground white pepper

8 oz pancetta

Method/Roasted Pheasant

Remove the skin from the pheasant breast, then butterfly the breast and use a meat mallet to pound to 1/4-inch thickness.

Combine sage, thyme, shallots and oil and rub on both sides of the breast.

Slice the pancetta into 16 very thin pieces.

Lay 8 pieces of pancetta on each piece of pheasant breast, leaving the edges of the breast pieces uncovered. Season with salt and pepper. Fold the edges in slightly, then tightly roll each breast piece with plastic wrap. Twist ends of wrap in opposite directions to remove any excess air. Put roll into foil and wrap tightly, twisting edges shut.

Place wrapped pheasant on a sheet pan and bake at 325° for 20 minutes or until internal temp is 150°.

Once cooked, unwrap pheasant pieces from foil and plastic and hold hot until service.

Ingredients/Roasted Apple

2 Red Delicious apples

3 sage leaves, chopped

2 shallots, finely diced

2 tsp olive oil

kosher salt

white pepper

Method/Roasted Apple

Peel, core and dice apples into 40 1/2-inch pieces.

Toss ingredients together and roast in 400° oven for 14 minutes or until apple is tender and golden brown.

Remove apple from the oven, chill and reserve.

Assembly

Slice each pheasant roulade into 10 even pieces.

On each skewer, place one piece of apple, followed by a piece of the roulade, then a second piece of apple.

Chef Note

The flavor profile for this item is very intense, so no sauce is needed. But if you want to add one, here's an easy recipe:

1 cup sour cream; 1/2 cup applesauce; 1 tsp apple vinegar. Whisk all together.

Variations

For a less expensive option, use pork loin instead of pheasant and smoked apple bacon instead of pancetta.

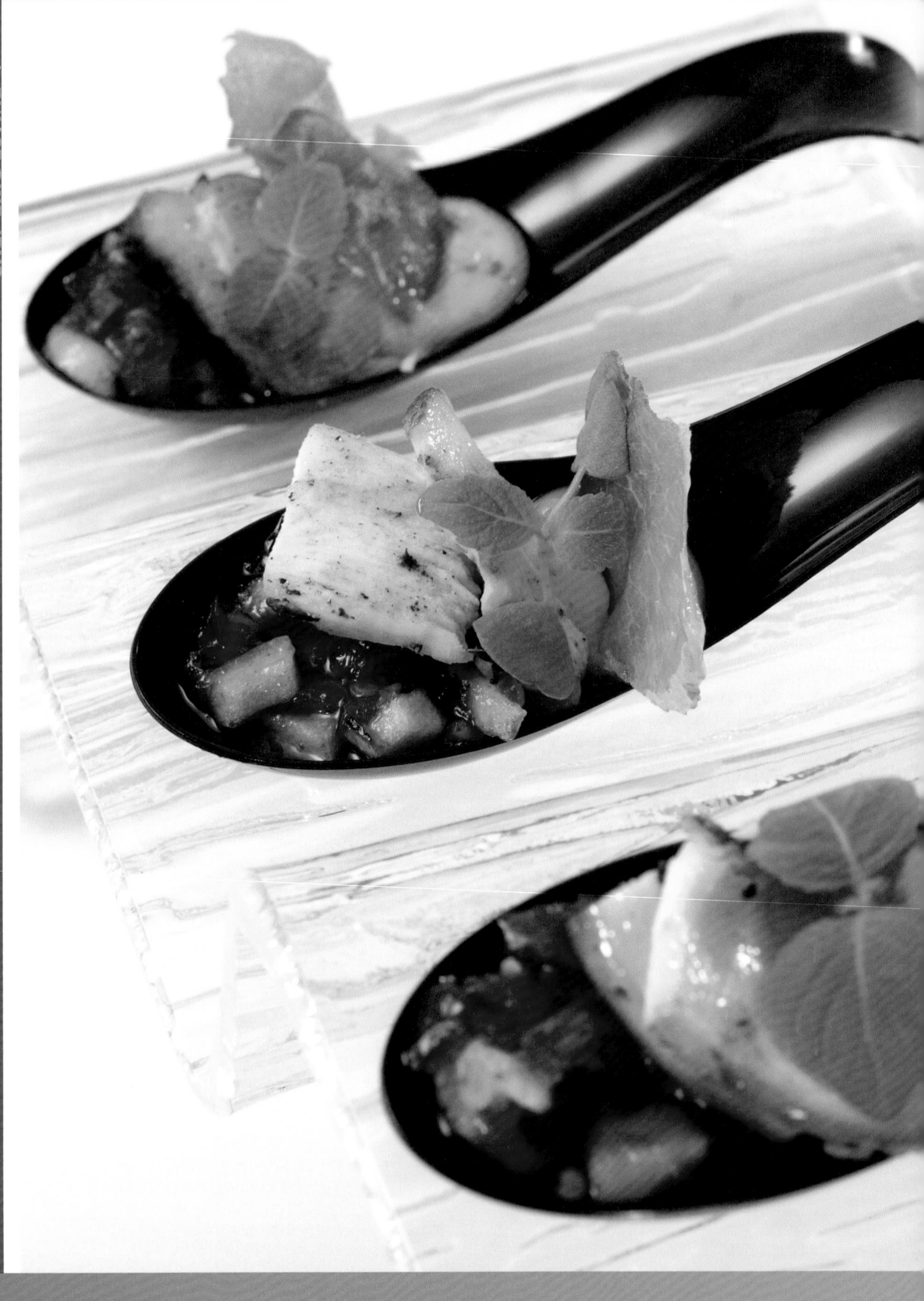

Makes about 10 servings

Grilled Pheasant with Apple Chutney and Prosciutto Crisps

Ingredients/Grilled Pheasant

2 pieces pheasant breast

2 tsp olive oil

2 sprigs fresh thyme, finely chopped

2 sprigs fresh sage, finely chopped

2 shallots, finely chopped

kosher salt

white pepper

Method/Grilled Pheasant

Rub pheasant pieces with olive oil, then rub with seasonings.

Grill breast pieces skin side down for 8 minutes, then turn and grill the other side until done, another 6 minutes.

Let breast pieces rest for 4 minutes, then cut into thin slices and set aside.

Ingredients/Apple Chutney

2 Granny Smith apples

1/2 cup chopped onion

1/4 cup red wine vinegar

1/4 cup brown sugar

1 Tbsp grated orange peel

1 Tbsp grated fresh ginger

1/2 tsp allspice

Method/Apple Chutney

Peel, core and chop apples, then combine all ingredients in a medium saucepan and stir well. Bring to a boil; reduce heat and simmer, covered, for 50 minutes.

Uncover and simmer over low heat for an additional 8 minutes to cook off excess liquid; let cool.

Ingredients/Prosciutto Crisps

4 pieces of paper-thin prosciutto

Method/Prosciutto Crisps

Place prosciutto slices on a sheet pan covered with parchment paper.

Bake at 325° for 5 minutes, or until prosciutto is crisp.

Cool before using.

Assembly

Place 1 tsp of apple chutney on each spoon, then top with 1 tsp sliced pheasant breast.

Crack Prosciutto Crisps into strips and stand vertically in each spoon.

Chef Notes
Give this dish a little heat by adding 1/2 tsp of red pepper flakes to the chutney while cooking the apple.

Variations
For a less expensive hors d'oeuvre, grill pork loin instead of pheasant.

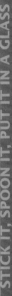

Pheasant, Apple, Pork

Chef Notes
*Drain the pork well; the idea is to slow roast,
not steam, the pork.*

Variations
*Pork loin can be used instead of pheasant or quail,
for a more familiar option. Try a ginger-mint mousse
instead of apple, for a different taste.*

POULTRY SENSATIONS

Makes about 10 servings

Poached Pheasant with Apple Mousse and Crispy Pork Belly

Ingredients/Poached Pheasant Breasts

2 pheasant breasts

2 shallots, chopped rough

2 tsp olive oil

2 cups pheasant stock

1 cup apple juice

1/2 bunch sage, chopped rough

Method/Poached Pheasant Breasts

Sauté shallots and sage in olive oil in a 1-qt pot, then add stock and apple juice.

Remove the skin from the pheasant breasts and add breasts to the pot.

Heat saucepan with pheasant breast to 160°, then reduce the heat and cook for 20 minutes, until the pheasant reaches an internal temperature of 150°.

Remove breasts from pot, cool and set aside.

Ingredients/Apple Mousse

1 Granny Smith apple

1/2 cup heavy cream

1/2 cup crème fraiche

1/4 bunch sage, finely chopped

kosher salt

white pepper

Method/Apple Mousse

Peel and core apple. Grate apple, using the small side of a grater.

Combine heavy cream and crème fraiche in a bowl and whisk by hand until the mixture is light and foamy.

Add chopped sage, apple, salt and pepper to the liquid. Refrigerate.

Ingredients/Crispy Pork Belly

2 lbs pork belly

1 cup granulated sugar

8 tsp salt

7 juniper berries

7 whole cloves

7 black peppercorns

1 bay leaf

4 qts water

2 onions, chopped

olive oil

salt

Method/Crispy Pork Belly

Place the sugar, 8 tsp salt, juniper berries, cloves, peppercorns, bay leaf and water in a pot and bring to a boil over high heat until the sugar and salt are dissolved. Pour the brine into a non-reactive container (food-grade plastic or stainless steel) and allow to cool completely, then put the pork belly into the brine. Make sure the pork belly is fully covered by the brine.

Cover and refrigerate for at least 8 hours and up to 3 days.

Drain the pork belly and pat it dry with paper towels. Using a very sharp knife or a box cutter, score the rind.

Rub the rind with olive oil and sprinkle with a pinch of salt. Place the chopped onions in the center of a roasting pan or cast iron skillet and set the pork belly on top of them.

Roast the pork belly on a rack in the upper third of the oven at 375° for 1-1/2 to 2 hours.

If the rind isn't as crisp as you'd like, finish by broiling the pork belly under high heat, moving it several times so the skin is evenly crisped.

Let the pork belly rest for 15–30 minutes, then cut into 20 pieces (1x1/2 inches)

Assembly

Shred the poached pheasant breasts with a fork and distribute evenly in service cups or glasses. Spoon 1/2 tsp Apple Mousse into each service cup.

Place two pieces of Crispy Pork Belly on top of the Apple Mousse, then top with another 1/2 tsp Apple Mousse.

Meat
REVELATIONS

BEEF SHORT RIBS ◆ CORN ◆ MUSHROOMS

PORK LOIN ◆ APPLES ◆ SAGE

VEAL ◆ CREMINI MUSHROOMS ◆ PEARL ONIONS

LAMB ◆ SCALLIONS ◆ YUKON GOLD POTATOES

There's nothing quite like the taste of perfectly prepared meat, but you don't have to serve up a T-bone steak to make people happy. A bite or two of meat, with the perfect accompanying flavors, is enough.

The recipes in this section nicely show off the flavors of beef, pork, veal and lamb. The preparations may start with familiar, homey ideas, like Shepherd's Pie or Braised Short Ribs, but every one of them adds something new and interesting (Five-Spice Popcorn, Saffron Apple Garlic Mousse).

Meat REVELATIONS

BEEF SHORT RIBS ◆ CORN ◆ MUSHROOMS

PORK LOIN ◆ APPLES ◆ SAGE

VEAL ◆ CREMINI MUSHROOMS ◆ PEARL ONIONS

LAMB ◆ SCALLIONS ◆ YUKON GOLD POTATOES

BBQ Short Ribs with
Grilled Corn and
Marinated Portobello
Mushrooms

Red Wine Braised
Short Ribs with Corn
Polenta and Cremini
Mushroom Chips

Asian Braised Short
Ribs with Stir-Fried
Mushrooms and
Five-Spice Popcorn

82

84

86

Ingredients/BBQ Short Ribs

3 lbs boneless beef short ribs

kosher salt

freshly ground black pepper

1/4 cup olive oil

1 large onion, diced

3 cloves garlic, coarsely chopped

1 cup tomato paste

1 cup red wine (cabernet sauvignon is good)

1/2 cup Dijon mustard

2 cups BBQ sauce

2 cups beef stock

Method/BBQ Short Ribs

Season the ribs with salt and pepper.

Heat the oil in a large heavy-bottomed pan over medium heat. Add the ribs in batches and brown on all sides, about 8–10 minutes. Remove browned ribs from pan and set aside.

Add the onion and garlic to the pan and cook, stirring frequently, for 2 minutes. Add the tomatoes, wine and mustard. Bring the mixture to a boil, scraping the brown bits from the ribs into the mixture.

Return the ribs to the pan and add the beef stock. Cover the pan and cook in a 300° oven for 2-1/2 hours, until the meat falls off the bone.

Remove the ribs from the pan and remove any excess fat from the surface of the cooking liquid.

Transfer the cooking liquid to the bowl of a food processor. Process until the mixture is a smooth sauce. Pour the sauce into a pan and keep warm over low heat

Ingredients/Grilled Corn

2 ears of corn, still in husks

kosher salt

3 oz butter

BBQ Short Ribs with Grilled Corn and Marinated Portobello Mushrooms

Method/Grilled Corn

Peel back the outer husk of the corn without actually removing it; remove the inner silky threads. Soak the ears in water for 10 minutes, then brush with butter, sprinkle with salt and wrap the outer husk back around the ear. Place on a preheated grill and grill for 15–20 minutes, until the corn is tender.

Ingredients/Marinated Portobello Mushrooms

2 portobello mushrooms

2 tsp olive oil

1 tsp minced garlic

kosher salt

white pepper

Method/Marinated Portobello Mushrooms

Remove the stems from the portobello mushrooms caps and cut the bottom parts off the stems, discarding any dirty portions.

Toss portobello into oil, garlic salt and pepper. Grill mushroom pieces until tender on a grill at medium temperature. Hold at room temperature until ready to use.

Ingredients/BBQ Sauce

2 tsp olive oil

6 garlic cloves, chopped

2 Tbsp tomato paste

1 Tbsp chili powder

1 Tbsp paprika

1 tsp crushed red pepper

1/2 tsp ground allspice

pinch ground cloves

2 cups ketchup

2 cups water

1/2 cup cider vinegar

1/4 cup dark molasses

1/4 cup firmly packed dark brown sugar

1 Tbsp kosher salt

1 Tbsp soy sauce

1 Tbsp Worcestershire sauce

2 tsp English-style dried mustard

1 tsp freshly ground black pepper

1 bay leaf

Method/BBQ Sauce

Heat the oil in a medium saucepan over medium heat. Stir in the garlic, tomato paste, chili powder, paprika, red pepper, allspice and cloves; cook, stirring, until a dark red paste forms, about 3 minutes.

Add the ketchup, water, vinegar, molasses, brown sugar, salt, soy sauce, Worcestershire, dried-mustard, black pepper and bay leaf.

Adjust the heat to maintain a gentle simmer and cook until the flavors come together, about 30 minutes.

Assembly

Cut the portobello mushroom caps into 1/2-inch pieces and the short ribs into 1-inch pieces. Cut the Grilled Corn into 1-inch pieces.

On each skewer, put one piece of portobello mushroom and then one piece of short rib. Finish the skewer with a piece of corn on the end.

Drizzle BBQ Sauce over each skewer before service.

Chef Notes

All of the components for this hors d'oeuvre can be prepared ahead of time, with assembly done on-site.

Short ribs are best prepared at least one day ahead. This allows the flavors to continue to develop while the short ribs sit in the sauce.

Variations

Instead of short ribs, try roasted pork loin or chili-lime chicken.

Chef Notes
Hold the polenta and short ribs at high temperatures before service, so it will stay hot as it is passed.

Variations
Any meat that is cooked long and slow is a great accompaniment to polenta; try slow-roasted pork loin, beef brisket or braised veal shank instead of short ribs.

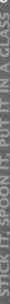

Red Wine Braised Short Ribs with Corn Polenta and Cremini Mushroom Chips

Ingredients/Red Wine Braised Short Ribs

3 lbs boneless beef short ribs

kosher salt

freshly ground black pepper

1/4 cup olive oil

1 large onion, diced

3 cloves garlic, coarsely chopped

1 cup tomato paste

1 cup red wine (cabernet sauvignon)

3 Tbsp Dijon mustard

2 cups beef stock

Method/Red Wine Braised Short Ribs

Season the ribs with salt and pepper. Heat the oil over medium heat in a large, heavy-bottomed pan. Add the ribs in batches and brown on all sides, about 8–10 minutes. Remove the ribs from pan and set aside.

Add the onion and garlic to the pan and cook, stirring frequently, for 2 minutes. Add the tomatoes, wine and mustard to the pan and bring the mixture to a boil, scraping up the brown bits that cling to the bottom of the pan with a wooden spoon.

Return the ribs to the pan. Add the beef stock to the pan, cover and roast at 325° for 2-1/2 hours, until the meat falls easily from the bone.

Remove the ribs from the pan and remove any excess fat from the surface of the cooking liquid.

Transfer the cooking liquid to the bowl of a food processor. Process until the mixture is a smooth sauce. Pour the sauce into a pan and keep warm over low heat.

Ingredients/Corn Polenta

1/4 lb unsalted butter

1/4 cup olive oil

3 cloves garlic

1 tsp crushed red pepper flakes

1 tsp minced fresh rosemary leaves

1/2 tsp kosher salt

1/2 tsp freshly ground black pepper

3 cups chicken stock, preferably homemade

2 cups half-and-half

2 cups milk

2 cups cornmeal

1 cup fresh corn kernels

1/2 cup grated Parmesan cheese

Method/Corn Polenta

Heat the butter and olive oil in a large saucepan. Add the garlic, red pepper flakes, rosemary, salt and pepper and sauté for 1 minute. Add the chicken stock, corn, half-and-half and milk and bring to a boil.

Remove the pan from the heat and slowly sprinkle the cornmeal into the hot milk while stirring constantly with a whisk.

Put the pan back on the stove and cook over low heat, stirring constantly, until thickened and bubbly, 5–7 minutes.

Remove from heat and add Parmesan. Hold hot until ready to serve.

Ingredients/Cremini Mushroom Chips

1/2 lb cremini mushrooms

kosher salt

Method/Cremini Mushroom Chips

Slice mushrooms 1/4-inch thick and sprinkle with salt.

Dry the mushroom slices in a dehydrator for 8 hours, or put in a 125° oven for 1/2 hour, then turn off the heat but leave the mushrooms in the oven for 11 hours. (If your oven has a pilot light, you can leave the mushroom slices in the oven for 12 hours with just the pilot light on.)

Assembly

Spoon polenta into ceramic spoons. Cut the short ribs into 1/2-inch pieces and place on the polenta. Drizzle 1/2 tsp of sauce on top of the meat just before service.

Top with mushroom chips and garnish with chives.

Chef Notes

The short ribs will be more flavorful if they are made the day before and reheated before service

The stir-fry vegetables should be cooked at the last moment to ensure they are tender.

Variations

Use curry, cilantro or star anise in the popcorn to complement the Asian flavor of the hors d'oeuvre.

Asian Braised Short Ribs with Stir-Fried Mushrooms and Five-Spice Popcorn

Ingredients/Asian Braised Short Ribs

3 lbs beef short ribs

1 cup soy sauce

1/4 cup rice wine vinegar

3 cloves garlic, chopped

1 (5-inch) stalk lemongrass, halved lengthwise and chopped

1 tsp freshly minced ginger

1/2 cup light brown sugar

1 qt water

1/2 cup green onions

3/4 tsp crushed red pepper

1/4 cup fresh orange juice

1/4 cup hoisin sauce

2 Tbsp fresh lemon juice

1 Tbsp soy sauce

1 tsp sesame oil

1 Tbsp cooking oil

1/2 tsp minced garlic

1/2 tsp minced ginger

1/2 cup julienned carrots

1/2 cup thinly sliced lotus root

1/2 cup julienned zucchini

1/2 cup julienned jicama

8 white button mushrooms, sliced

2 Tbsp water

1/2 cup julienned red bell pepper

4 asparagus spears, sliced in bias-cut pieces

2 tsp cornstarch dissolved in 1 Tbsp water

Method/Asian Braised Short Ribs

Cut the short ribs into 4-oz portions

In a wide stockpot or Dutch oven, combine the short ribs, soy sauce, vinegar, garlic, lemongrass, ginger, brown sugar, water, green onion bottoms, crushed red pepper and 2 Tbsp of orange juice. Make sure the stockpot is deep enough so the short ribs can be fully submerged in the liquid. Cover the pot.

Bake the short ribs in a 350° oven for about 3 hours, or until the meat is tender and falling off the bones. Remove the short ribs from the braising liquid and cover to keep warm.

Remove the fat from the top of the cooking liquid and discard.

Place the remaining braising juices in a medium saucepan with 1/4 cup of the hoisin sauce; bring to a boil over medium-high heat. Reduce the liquid until only about 1-1/4 cups remain, about 20 minutes, then pour through a fine-meshed strainer, discarding the solids. Stir in the remaining 2 Tbsp of orange juice and the lemon juice.

Return the short ribs and the reduced sauce to the stockpot or Dutch oven; coat the short ribs with the sauce.

Bake uncovered for 10 minutes at 425°, until the short ribs are heated through and slightly glazed.

Set aside until ready to serve.

Ingredients/Stir-Fried Mushrooms

1/2 cup vegetable broth

1 Tbsp Chinese rice wine or dry sherry

Method/Stir-Fried Mushrooms

Combine vegetable broth, rice wine and soy sauce in a bowl.

Place a wok over high heat until it is hot. Add the sesame and cooking oil and swirl it in the wok, to coat all sides of the pan.

Add the garlic and ginger to the wok and stir to release their fragrance, about 10 seconds. Add the carrots, lotus root, jicama, zucchini and mushrooms; stir-fry for about a minute.

Add the 2 Tbsp water to the wok, cover and let cook for 3 minutes. Add the red bell pepper and asparagus pieces and stir-fry for 1 minute.

Add the vegetable broth sauce and bring to a boil, then add the cornstarch solution and cook, stirring constantly, until the sauce boils and thickens.

Ingredients/Five-Spice Popcorn

1/2 cup unpopped popcorn

3 tsp five-spice powder

sesame oil

Method/Five-Spice Popcorn

Pop the corn, using sesame oil, then toss with five-spice powder. Set aside.

Assembly

Place stir fry at bottom of the cup, place short ribs with sauce on top of stir fry and finish with popcorn; garnish with chive flower.

Meat
REVELATIONS

BEEF SHORT RIBS ◆ CORN ◆ MUSHROOMS

PORK LOIN ◆ APPLES ◆ SAGE

VEAL ◆ CREMINI MUSHROOMS ◆ PEARL ONIONS

LAMB ◆ SCALLIONS ◆ YUKON GOLD POTATOES

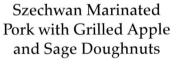

Stick

Spoon

Glass

Szechwan Marinated
Pork with Grilled Apple
and Sage Doughnuts

Sweet and Sour Pork
Dumplings with
Ginger Apple Glaze
and Sage Dust

Crispy Pork Loin with
Saffron Apple Garlic
Mousse and
Sage Crisps

90

92

94

Pork Loin, Apples, Sage

Chef Notes
You can use less sugar in the doughnut, if you wish. This will create a savory flavor profile, with the sage standing out more.

Variations
Braised chicken thighs are a good—and less expensive—substitute for the pork. The thighs, an often under-used part of the chicken, can be braised in a sauce of red wine, chicken demi-glace, rosemary and garlic for great flavor contrast.

Ingredients/Szechwan Marinated Pork

2 lbs pork loin
1/2 cup soy sauce
1 Tbsp honey
1 tsp chili flakes
1/2 tsp ground cumin
1/2 tsp turmeric
6 Tbsp unsalted butter
2 garlic cloves, finely chopped
1 green onion, finely chopped
1 cup veal or chicken stock
1/4 cup soy sauce
1 Tbsp chili flakes

Method/Szechwan Marinated Pork

In a small bowl, combine the soy sauce, honey, chili flakes, cumin and turmeric and pour over the meat, turning to coat all sides.

Let the pork loin marinate at room temperature for about 15 minutes.

In a small skillet, melt 2 Tbsp butter. Add the garlic and green onion and sauté over medium-high heat until soft, about 2 minutes.

Makes about 20 servings

Szechwan Marinated Pork with Grilled Apple and Sage Doughnuts

Pour the stock, soy sauce, and chili flakes into the skillet and cook 1 or 2 minutes longer.

Strain the sauce into a clean pan and whisk in the remaining 4 Tbsp butter. Keep warm until service.

On an outdoor or kitchen grill, cook the pork loin about 6 minutes on each side until the internal temperature reaches 160°. After grilling, cut the pork loin into 1-inch cubes.

Ingredients/Grilled Apple

1 Granny Smith apple

2 tsp olive oil

kosher salt

white pepper

Method/Grilled Apple

Core apple and cut into 1-inch chunks. Toss apple chunks with salt, pepper and oil.

Grill the apple pieces until tender on an open grill. Set aside.

Ingredients/Sage Doughnuts

1-1/2 cups milk

2-1/2 oz (about 1/3 cup) vegetable shortening

2 packets instant yeast

1/3 cup warm water (95° to 105°)

2 eggs, beaten

1/4 cup sugar

1-1/2 tsp salt

1 tsp freshly ground nutmeg

1 cup all-purpose flour, plus more for dusting surface

peanut or vegetable oil for frying (1 to 1-1/2 gal, depending on fryer)

3 tsp fresh sage

salt

pepper

Method

Put the milk in a medium saucepan and heat over medium heat until just warm enough to melt shortening. Put the shortening in a bowl and pour the warmed milk over. Set aside.

In a small bowl, sprinkle the yeast over the warm water and let dissolve for 5 minutes, then pour the yeast mixture into the large bowl of a stand mixer and add the milk and shortening mixture, first making sure the milk and shortening have cooled to lukewarm.

Add the eggs, sugar, salt, nutmeg and half the flour. Using the paddle attachment for the mixer, combine the ingredients on low speed until the flour is incorporated; then increase the speed to medium and beat until ingredients are well combined, about 2-3 minutes.

Add the remaining flour, beating on low speed at first, then increasing the speed to medium and beating for 2 minutes.

Using the dough hook attachment of the mixer, beat the dough at medium speed until it pulls away from the sides of the bowl and becomes smooth, about 2–3 minutes.

Add the sage to the dough and mix for 1–2 minutes more.

Transfer dough to a well-oiled bowl; cover and let rise for 1 hour or until doubled in size.

On a well-floured surface, roll dough out to 3/8-inch thick.

Cut 20 doughnuts, using a 1-1/2-inch doughnut cutter or pastry ring and a 4/8-inch ring for the center hole. Set doughnuts on a floured baking sheet and cover lightly with a tea towel; let rise for 30 minutes.

Using a deep fryer at 365°, gently place doughnuts into the hot oil, 3-4 at a time. Cook for 1 minute per side, then transfer doughnuts to a cooling rack set on a baking pan. Season doughnuts with salt and pepper.

Allow doughnuts to cool 15–20 minutes before using.

Assembly

Put one Sage Doughnut on each skewer, followed by a piece of apple, then a piece of pork loin. Then put another piece of apple on the skewer.

Chef Notes

The dumplings can be made ahead of time and frozen for
use. Before serving, remove the dumplings from the freez
let sit at room temperature until they are fully thawed an

Variations

Chicken, shrimp or scallops can be used to replace
the pork in the dumpling filling. For a Latin flavor,
use cilantro, fresh chiles, lime and black bean
purée instead of the Ginger Glaze.

Makes about 20 servings

Sweet and Sour Pork Dumplings with Ginger Apple Glaze and Sage Dust

Ingredients/Pork Dumplings

1 lb ground pork

1 (5-oz) can water chestnuts, drained and chopped

1/2 cup scallions

1 tsp chopped garlic

1 tsp minced ginger

1 tsp sesame oil

1 egg, beaten

1 pack Oriental sesame dressing mix

2 Tbsp oyster sauce

1 (16-oz) pack 4x4-inch wonton wrappers

savoy or napa cabbage

Method/Pork Dumplings

In a large bowl, mix the pork, water chestnuts, scallions, garlic, ginger, sesame oil, egg, sesame dressing mix and oyster sauce.

Fill center of each wonton wrapper with 1 tsp of the meat filling. Brush the edges with water to help seal. Gather the corners of the wonton wrapper to the center and twist to secure.

Arrange the cabbage leaves on the bottom of a bamboo steamer and place the dumplings about 1-inch apart on the cabbage leaves. Steam the dumplings about 20 minutes, until the filling is fully cooked.

Ingredients/Ginger Apple Glaze

3 Tbsp canola oil

3 shallots, finely chopped

3 garlic cloves, finely chopped

2 Thai chilies, seeded and chopped

1 oz fresh ginger

2 Tbsp curry powder

1 tsp ground cinnamon

2 star anise, grated

3 apples, cored, peeled and cut into chunks

1 cup apple juice

1/4 cup hoisin sauce

2 Tbsp soy sauce

1/4 cup honey

1/4 cup light brown sugar

2 Tbsp grated fresh ginger

1 cup water

Method/Ginger Apple Glaze

Heat the oil in a large non-reactive saucepan over medium heat. Add the shallots and garlic and cook until soft. Add the Thai chiles, ginger, curry powder and cinnamon and cook for 2 minutes.

Add the remaining ingredients and 1 cup of water. Cook until the sauce is reduced and thickened, 30–40 minutes, stirring occasionally. Remove from heat and let cool slightly.

Process the apple mixture until smooth, working in two or three batches. Strain into a bowl after processing.

Let glaze cool to room temperature and set aside.

Ingredients/Sage Dust

1 bunch fresh sage

1/2 cup panko breadcrumbs

kosher salt

Method/Sage Dust

Place sage leaves in a dehydrator at 130° for 6–8 hours. (If you don't have a dehydrator, lay the sage leaves on a sheet pan and bake in a 180° oven for 1 hour or until crisp.)

Put the dried sage leaves in a food processor and process, slowly adding the breadcrumbs and salt as you do. Process until you have fine sage "dust." Set aside until service.

Assembly

Put a dumpling in each spoon, top with Ginger Glaze and then sprinkle with Sage Dust just before service.

Chef Notes

The saffron mousse can be prepared the day before. Depending on the fat content of the cream, you may need to add extra cream cheese to help stabilize the mixture if you are making it ahead of time.

Variations

Chicken or shrimp can be used instead of pork. Make a five-spice mousse and garnish with a crispy scallion and cilantro mixture.

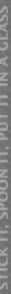

Crispy Pork Loin with Saffron Apple Garlic Mousse and Sage Crisps

Ingredients/Crispy Pork Loin

2 lbs pork loin

1–1/2 cups panko breadcrumbs

1 Tbsp curry powder

1 Tbsp ground fennel

1 tsp dried sage

1 tsp dried thyme

1 tsp garlic powder

1 tsp dried parsley

2 tsp kosher salt

2 tsp freshly ground black pepper

1 cup all-purpose flour

2 eggs, beaten

3 Tbsp olive oil

Method/Crispy Pork Loin

Cut the pork loin into 2-inch chunks. Combine the panko breadcrumbs and the seasonings in a medium bowl. Put the flour in another bowl and the eggs in another. Dip the pork pieces in the flour, then the egg, then the breadcrumb mix.

Heat half the oil in a sauté pan over high heat; sear half of the breaded pork until golden brown on all sides, about 5 minutes, then transfer the pork to a sheet pan. Repeat with the remaining oil and pork.

Bake the pork in a 400° oven for 3–5 minutes for medium-cooked pork.

Ingredients/Saffron Apple Garlic Mousse

1 cup heavy cream

1/4 lb cream cheese

1 Granny Smith apple

3 garlic cloves

1 tsp olive oil

kosher salt

white pepper

1 tsp saffron threads

2 tsp warm water

Method/Saffron Apple Garlic Mousse

Using an electric mixer, combine the whipping cream and cream cheese in a bowl and whip on high speed until hard peaks form.

In small bowl, crumble the saffron threads in the warm water to extract the saffron essence.

Peel, core and grate the apple into the cream mixture.

Toss the garlic cloves into olive oil, salt and pepper and roast at 350° until the garlic is soft and brown, 35-40 minutes.

Remove the garlic from the oven and smash each clove with the side of a knife until the garlic has a texture like paste. Add garlic to the bowl of whipped cream and cream cheese. Add the saffron liquid to the bowl and fold into the mixture until it's fully incorporated. Set aside.

Ingredients/Sage Crisps

10 sage leaves

kosher salt

oil

Method/Sage Crisps

In a fryer, cook the sage leaves until they are crisp and slightly transparent. Remove from fryer and sprinkle with salt. Set aside.

Assembly

Alternate pieces of Crispy Pork Loin and dollops of saffron mousse in each service cup or glass. End with mousse, then garnish with a Sage Crisp.

BEEF SHORT RIBS ◆ CORN ◆ MUSHROOMS

PORK LOIN ◆ APPLES ◆ SAGE

VEAL ◆ CREMINI MUSHROOMS ◆ PEARL ONIONS

LAMB ◆ SCALLIONS ◆ YUKON GOLD POTATOES

Veal Sweetbreads with Cremini Mushroom Custard and Roasted Cherry Tomatoes

98

Pan Roasted Veal Loin with Grilled Cremini Mushrooms and Crispy Shallots

100

Veal Shepherd's Pie with Cremini Mushroom Mashed Potatoes and Caramelized Onion Sauce

102

Veal, Cremini Mushrooms, Onions

Chef Notes
The custard must be thick enough to stay on skewers.

*Sweetbreads are amazing. They are not commonly used
but I believe this recipe will change your guests'
impression of this tasty treat*

Variations
*Substitute the sweetbreads with veal loin,
pork loin or even chicken.*

Veal Sweetbreads with Cremini Mushroom Custard and Roasted Cherry Tomatoes

Ingredients/Veal Sweetbreads

1 veal sweetbread

2 cups instant (Wondra) flour

2 cups milk

kosher salt

freshly ground black pepper

3 tsp olive oil

Method/Veal Sweetbreads

Remove inner membrane and vein of sweetbread. Cut sweetbread into 20 even pieces and soak them in milk for 1 hour.

Remove sweetbreads from milk and let drain, then roll in flour seasoned with salt and pepper.

Heat sauté pan and add olive oil. Sauté floured sweetbread pieces until golden brown and still tender inside, about 7-8 minutes, then season with salt and pepper. Reserve, keeping warm, until ready to skewer.

Ingredients/Cremini Mushroom Custard

1 cup heavy cream

5 egg yolks

kosher salt

ground white pepper

2 tsp olive oil

2 shallots, chopped

6 oz fresh cremini mushrooms, sliced

1 bunch fresh thyme, chopped

Method/Cremini Mushroom Custard

Sauté shallots and thyme in olive oil; add sliced mushrooms and season with salt and pepper. When vegetables are sautéed, put into a blender and purée until smooth.

Slowly add heavy cream to the mushroom mixture, then incorporate egg yolks, one at a time.

Pour custard in 1 oz ramekins and put ramekins into a water bath, then bake in 325° oven for 20 minutes, until custard is firm.

Cool and set aside.

Ingredients/Crispy Onions

1 Spanish onion

2 cups instant (Wondra) flour

1 cup buttermilk

2 qts oil for frying

Method

Shave onions and place into buttermilk for 30 minutes. Remove from milk and dredge in flour.

Quickly fry and reserve on paper towel to drain oil before use.

Ingredients/Roasted Cherry Tomatoes

10 cherry tomatoes

3 garlic cloves

3 tsp olive oil

kosher salt

ground white pepper

Method/Roasted Cherry Tomatoes

Sauté garlic cloves in olive oil until light brown, then add tomatoes and sauté until tender; season with salt and pepper.

Cool and set aside.

Assembly

Place food on skewers in this order: one piece of sweetbread, one cherry tomato, Crispy Onions, one piece of custard.

Warm slightly before service; this dish should be served at room temperature.

Chef Notes
This item should be served hot for the best flavor, so speed of service must be timed well in order to execute the dish properly.

Variations
Wild boar has a strong game-meat taste that balances well with the mushrooms and shallots. Venison or ostrich upscales the dish and makes it almost exotic. Both venison and ostrich have less fat than veal and lack marbleization, so be careful not to overcook.

Makes about 10 servings

Pan Roasted Veal Loin with Grilled Cremini Mushrooms and Crispy Shallots

Ingredients/Grilled Veal Loin

1 lb veal loin

kosher salt

freshly ground black pepper

3 tsp olive oil

Method/Grilled Veal Loin

Trim excess fat off veal loin and season loin with salt and pepper. Add olive oil to a sauté pan and sear veal for 2-3 minutes on each side.

Cook veal loin in 350° oven for 20 minutes, or until it reaches an internal temperature of 125°.

Remove loin from pan and let rest before slicing.

Ingredients/Cremini Mushrooms

10 cremini mushrooms, sliced in ½-inch pieces

2 cloves garlic, chopped

3 tsp olive oil

1/2 bunch fresh thyme, chopped

kosher salt

white pepper

Method/Cremini Mushrooms

Toss the mushrooms with thyme, garlic, salt, pepper and olive oil. Grill on an open grill until the mushrooms are tender, about 3 minutes, then set aside and keep warm.

Ingredients/Crispy Shallots

3 shallots, shaved on a mandoline or Chinese slicer

1 cup buttermilk

2 cups instant (Wondra) flour

1/2 bunch fresh thyme leaves (remove stems), finely chopped

kosher salt

white pepper

1 qt oil for frying

Method/Crispy Shallots

Soak the shallots in the buttermilk for 20 minutes, then drain. Dredge shallot shavings, a small batch at a time, in the flour.

Fry the shallots in oil at 325° until they are crisp; remove from the fryer and lay on paper towels to drain. Season immediately with thyme, salt and pepper.

Ingredients/Red Wine Reduction

3 cups burgundy cooking wine

1 cup pork stock

4 oz tomato paste

2 tsp olive oil

3 shallots, roughly chopped

1 bunch fresh thyme leaves (remove stems), roughly chopped

Method/Red Wine Reduction

Lightly sauté shallots and thyme. Add tomato paste to the pan and heat, then add the red wine. Reduce until the mixture is thick, about 10 minutes, then add pork stock and reduce again, about 20 minutes.

Strain the mixture when thickened and set aside.

Assembly

Slice the Grilled Veal Loin into 30 pieces.

Put some Red Wine Reduction in the spoon. Put 3 pieces of veal on top of the wine reduction, then add 1 or 2 pieces of mushroom. Top with fried shallots.

Ingredients/Veal Shepherd's Pie

1 Tbsp plus 1 tsp unsalted butter

1-1/2 cups diced onion

2 large cloves garlic, minced

2 tsp chopped fresh thyme leaves

2 lbs ground veal

1 tsp kosher salt, plus more as needed

1/4 tsp freshly ground black pepper, plus more as needed

3 Tbsp tomato paste

1 cup canned crushed tomatoes

1 bay leaf

3 Tbsp minced flat-leaf parsley leaves

3/4 lb turnips, cut into 1-inch pieces

3/4 lb carrots, cut into 1-inch pieces

2 tsp unsalted butter

1/2 tsp sugar

kosher salt

freshly ground pepper

1/4 cup grated farmhouse cheddar (optional)

Method/Veal Shepherd's Pie

In a large skillet, heat 1 Tbsp butter over medium heat. Add the onion and sauté, stirring frequently, until onion is golden, 10–12 minutes. Add the garlic and thyme and cook for 1 minute more. Add the meat, breaking it up with a wooden spoon, and cook until it loses its red color, about 5 minutes.

Add 1 tsp salt, 1/4 tsp pepper and the tomato paste and cook for 1 minute more.

Add the crushed tomatoes and bay leaf and bring to a simmer. Cover and cook for 20 minutes. Remove the bay leaf and spoon off any excess fat. Stir in the parsley and add salt and pepper to taste. Set aside.

Veal Shepherd's Pie with Cremini Mushroom Mashed Potatoes and Caramelized Onion Sauce

Put the turnips and carrots in a single layer in a skillet just large enough to hold them.

Add enough water so that it comes halfway up the sides of the vegetables; add 2 tsp unsalted butter and 1/2 tsp sugar. Bring to a boil over high heat, then adjust the heat to maintain a simmer.

Cover the vegetables with a round of parchment paper just large enough to fit the inside of the pan, or with a lid slightly ajar. Simmer the vegetables until tender, 8–10 minutes.

Remove the cover and raise the heat to high. Toss the vegetables frequently in the pan, as the liquid evaporates to a shiny smooth glaze. Season with salt and pepper to taste, then add to meat mixture. Set aside.

Ingredients/Cremini Mushroom Mashed Potatoes

1/2 lb button or cremini mushrooms, trimmed and quartered

2 lbs russet potatoes, peeled and cut into 1-inch pieces

1 tsp kosher salt

3/4 cup whole milk

1/4 cup plus 1 Tbsp unsalted butter

Freshly ground black pepper

Freshly grated nutmeg

Method/Cremini Mushroom Mashed Potatoes

Heat 1 Tbsp butter in a skillet over medium-high heat and sauté the mushrooms until golden, about 5 minutes. Season with salt and pepper, then set aside.

In a large saucepan, combine the potatoes, 1 tsp salt and cold water to cover. Bring to a boil over high heat. Lower the heat to maintain a simmer and cook until fork tender, about 10 minutes. Drain the potatoes and return to the pan. Shake the pan over medium heat for about a minute to dry the potatoes, then transfer the potatoes to a food mill, ricer or bowl.

Put the milk and butter in the saucepan and heat over medium-high heat until the milk is hot and the butter melts. Remove the pan from the heat. Mash the potatoes through the food mill or ricer, or by hand, into the pan. Stir to combine with the milk and butter. Season with salt and pepper and nutmeg, if desired. Add in sautéed mushrooms. Set aside.

Ingredients/Caramelized Onion Sauce

2 Tbsp olive oil

4 cups thinly sliced onions

salt

freshly ground black pepper

2 cups chicken stock

Method/Caramelized Onion Sauce

Put the oil in a saucepan over medium heat. When the oil is hot, add the onions and season with salt and pepper. Sauté for 10–12 minutes, or until caramelized.

Add the stock and bring to a boil. Reduce the heat to medium-low and simmer the sauce for 10 minutes. Remove from the heat and, using a hand-held blender, purée until smooth. Strain through a sieve and cool completely. Taste; season if necessary

Assembly

Scoop the meat and vegetable mixture into service cups or glasses. Add onion sauce, and then pipe the mashed potatoes on top.

Chef Notes
Wrap the piping bag filled with hot mashed potatoes in a towel, to keep from burning your hands.

Variations
Upscale the hors d'oeuvre by using ground seafood—shrimp, scallops or lobster—and then topping with wasabi mashed potatoes.

Meat

REVELATIONS

BEEF SHORT RIBS ◆ CORN ◆ MUSHROOMS

PORK LOIN ◆ APPLES ◆ SAGE

VEAL ◆ CREMINI MUSHROOMS ◆ PEARL ONIONS

LAMB ◆ SCALLIONS ◆ YUKON GOLD POTATOES

Oven Roasted Lamb
Loin with Roasted Yukon
Gold Potatoes, Grilled
Scallions and Chili Mint
Dipping Sauce

106

Grilled Lamb
with Pickled Scallions
and Poached Yukon
Potato Cubes

108

Lamb Sausage with
Stir-Fried Yukon
Potatoes and
Roasted Scallions

110

CHEF ERIC LeVINE

Chef Notes
This item is versatile; you can serve it hot or cold,
depending on the time of day and the event.

Variations
Create an interesting fall menu item by using
sweet potatoes and brisket or short ribs.

MEAT REVELATIONS

Oven Roasted Lamb Loin with Roasted Yukon Gold Potatoes, Grilled Scallions and Chili Mint Dipping Sauce

Ingredients/Roasted Lamb Loin

20 oz lamb loin

1/4 bunch fresh rosemary leaves, finely chopped

3 garlic cloves finely chopped

2 tsp olive oil

kosher salt

white pepper

Method/Roasted Lamb Loin

Trim any excess fat from the lamb loin. Mix the rosemary, garlic and olive oil and rub into the lamb loin. Season with salt and pepper.

Sear the lamb loin in a pan over high heat on all sides for 3 minutes minutes, then put in a 350° oven for 15 minutes or until the internal temperature is 125°.

Let the lamb cool and set aside.

Ingredients/Roasted Yukon Gold Potatoes

10 small Yukon gold potatoes

3 garlic cloves, chopped

2 tsp olive oil

1/4 bunch fresh rosemary leaves, chopped

1/2 bunch scallion greens, chopped; reserve whites for grilling

kosher salt

white pepper

Method/Roasted Yukon Gold Potatoes

Peel potatoes and cut into 1/2-inch cubes.

Toss potatoes with garlic, rosemary, scallions, oil, salt and pepper. Put potatoes on a sheet pan and roast at 350° for 20 minutes or until tender.

Remove potatoes from oven and chill before skewering.

Ingredients/Grilled Scallions

20 scallions, white portions cut in 1-1/2-inch pieces (from scallions used with potatoes)

2 tsp olive oil

kosher salt

white pepper

Method/Grilled Scallions

Season white portions of scallions with salt, pepper and oil.

Lightly grill scallions over a medium flame until they are almost tender.

Cool and set aside.

Ingredients/Chili Mint Dipping Sauce

1/2 cup duck sauce

1/2 cup plum sauce

1 tsp red pepper flakes

1/4 bunch fresh mint, finely chopped

2 limes

Method/Chili Mint Dipping Sauce

Combine the duck and plum sauces; add the red pepper flakes and mint and squeeze in the juice from the limes; mix thoroughly.

Assembly

Slice the lamb loin into 20 pieces. On each skewer, place one piece of lamb, one piece of scallion whites and one piece of potato, then another scallion.

Serve with the Chili Mint Dipping Sauce.

Makes about 20 servings

Grilled Lamb with Pickled Scallions and Poached Yukon Potato Cubes

Ingredients/Grilled Lamb Loin

20 oz lamb loin

1/4 bunch fresh rosemary leaves, finely chopped

3 garlic cloves finely chopped

2 tsp olive oil

kosher salt

white pepper

Method/Grilled Lamb Loin

Trim lamb loin of excess fat.

Mix the olive oil, rosemary and garlic and rub into lamb loin. Season with salt and pepper.

Grill the lamb loin on an open flame grill for 15 minutes or until it reaches an internal temperature of 125°.

Allow to rest before slicing.

Ingredients/Pickled Scallions

20 scallions, white portions only

1/2 cup orange juice

1/2 cup red wine vinegar

1/2 cup granulated sugar

Method/Pickled Scallions

Combine all ingredients, heat to 135° and let steep, like tea, for 30 minutes.

Cool and set aside, leaving scallions in the liquid until service.

Ingredients/Poached Yukon Gold Potato Cubes

10 small Yukon gold potatoes

3 garlic cloves, chopped

2 cups lamb or chicken stock

1/4 bunch fresh rosemary leaves, chopped

1/2 bunch scallion greens, chopped

kosher salt

white pepper

Method/Poached Yukon Gold Potato Cubes

Peel potatoes and cut into 1/2-inch cubes.

Place all ingredients in a pot with the stock and lightly poach until the potatoes are tender, about 12-15 minutes.

Remove potatoes and set aside.

Reduce the liquid in the pot until thick and viscous; set aside.

Assembly

Slice the lamb into 20 pieces.

Put potato cubes in each spoon, place lamb on top, then spoon poaching liquid over the lamb. Top with pickled scallions.

Chef Notes
Finish the lamb as close to service as possible, for the best flavor and texture.

Variations
All of the key components of this dish can be changed easily: Use leeks instead of scallions. Duck, veal or beef loin can be used instead of lamb. A potato foam, instead of the poached potato cubes, adds a note of surprise, while keeping the basic flavor.

Chef Notes
Stir the vegetables just before service to
keep them from getting overcooked.

Variations:
Lobster or chicken sausage instead of lamb can either
upscale or downscale this item. Instead of the stir-fried
vegetables in the recipe, try a combination of
Napa cabbage, wild mushrooms and shaved pearl
onions for an earthier flavor. Peruvian purple
potatoes or banana potatoes create an interesting
appearance, as well as new flavors.

MEAT REVELATIONS

Lamb Sausage with Stir-Fried Yukon Potatoes and Roasted Scallions

Ingredients/Poaching Liquid
8 cups beef broth

8 cups port wine

7 bay leaves

5 cinnamon sticks

1/4 cup whole peppercorns

1 onion, skin on, halved

3 tsp kosher salt

1 tsp ground nutmeg

1 tsp ground allspice

1 tsp ground cumin

Ingredients/Lamb Sausage
3 lbs ground leg of lamb

6 eggs

1 cup heavy cream

1/4 cup olive oil

3 cups shelled pistachios

1/4 cup chopped shallots

1/4 cup chopped garlic

1 cup finely chopped fresh rosemary leaves

1/4 cup port wine

1 tsp ground allspice

1 tsp ground cumin

1 tsp ground nutmeg

1 Tbsp kosher salt

1 tsp coarse ground black pepper

1-2 cups dried breadcrumbs

Method/Lamb Sausage
Put all ingredients for the poaching liquid in a shallow 3-qt pot and bring to a simmer.

Mix all the sausage ingredients except the breadcrumbs in a large bowl; add 1 to 2 cups breadcrumbs until the mixture forms a shape and doesn't stick to your hands.

Cut plastic wrap into 8x8-inch squares.

For each sausage, roll 2 Tbsp of mixture into a tube shape and roll into the plastic wrap, twisting the ends to create a tight sausage shape.

Cook one plastic-wrapped sausage in the boiling poaching liquid for approximately 20 minutes as a test, before making the rest of the sausages. Let the test sausage cool in the refrigerator for 15 minutes, then slice it to test consistency. If it falls apart, add more breadcrumbs to the sausage mixture and test another sausage.

Once the mixture is the proper texture, roll and poach the rest of the sausages. Set sausages aside.

Ingredients/Stir-Fried Yukon Potatoes
1 lb Yukon gold potatoes

1/2 red onion

1/2 cup snow peas

1/2 cup shiitake mushrooms

1/2 cup bean sprouts

1 tsp chopped fresh ginger

2 garlic cloves, chopped

2 tsp sesame oil

2 tsp Teriyaki sauce

scallion greens (from roasted scallions), chopped

Method/Stir-Fried Yukon Potatoes
Heat sesame oil in a wok, then add scallions, ginger and garlic.

Add the potatoes, onions, snow peas, mushrooms and bean sprouts and sauté until vegetables are slightly tender, about 3-5 minutes.

Add Teriyaki sauce to finish, then remove from heat and set aside.

Ingredients/Roasted Scallions
20 white portions from scallions

2 tsp sesame oil

kosher salt

white pepper

Method/Roasted Scallions
Season scallions with the salt, pepper and oil. Place on a sheet pan and roast at 350° until tender, about 7-10 minutes. Set aside.

Assembly
Spoon some stir-fried vegetables into each service cup.

Slice the lamb sausages into a total of 40 pieces and place 2 pieces into each cup.

Spoon a little more stir-fried vegetables over the lamb pieces, then top with a scallion.

CHAPTER FOUR

Vegetable INNOVATIONS

RADISH ◆ ENOKI MUSHROOMS ◆ TOMATO
EGGPLANT ◆ GARLIC ◆ RICOTTA
POTATO ◆ MUSHROOM ◆ ONION
BEETS ◆ GOAT CHEESE ◆ BALSAMIC VINEGAR

What could be more versatile than vegetables? They come in pretty much any color, size or flavor you can imagine. And chefs are constantly finding new uses for old favorites, like the radish, or "new" vegetables, like Peruvian potatoes.

Some of these hors d'oeuvre are strictly vegetarian, some include a taste of protein like crispy bacon pieces. All are delicious.

Vegetable

INNOVATIONS

RADISH ◆ ENOKI MUSHROOMS ◆ TOMATO
EGGPLANT ◆ GARLIC ◆ RICOTTA
POTATO ◆ MUSHROOM ◆ ONION
BEETS ◆ GOAT CHEESE ◆ BALSAMIC VINEGAR

Daikon Radish with
Roasted Tomatoes and
Tempura-Fried Enoki

Grilled Enoki
Mushrooms with
Tomato Gelée and
Radish Sprouts

Watermelon Radish
with Soy Scallion-
Marinated Tomatoes
and Marinated
Enoki Mushrooms

116

118

120

VEGETABLE INNOVATIONS

Makes about 10 servings

Daikon Radish with Roasted Tomatoes and Tempura-Fried Enoki

Ingredients/Marinated Daikon Radish

1 Daikon radish

1 cup rice wine vinegar

1/2 cup white soy paste

1 stalk lemongrass, chopped

1 red pepper, cut in 1/2-inch cubes

2 scallions, bias-cut into 1-inch pieces

3 tsp cornstarch

Method/Marinated Daikon Radish

Peel the skin from the radish; with a peeler, shave the radish paper-thin into 20 2-inch ribbons.

Put the lemongrass in the rice wine vinegar; add the soy paste and scallions.

Marinate the radish ribbons and pepper pieces in the liquid for 30 minutes. Remove the vegetables from the liquid just before service.

Heat the marinade from the radishes until it boils. Thicken with 3 tsp cornstarch that has been mixed with 2 Tbsp water. Use the thickened marinade as a dipping sauce for assembly.

Ingredients/Roasted Tomatoes

10 red pear tomatoes

10 yellow pear tomatoes

2 garlic cloves, finely chopped

2 tsp sesame oil

1/4 bunch scallions, sliced

1 tsp soy sauce

Method/Roasted Tomatoes

Toss all ingredients together in a bowl, then place on a sheet pan and roast in a 350° oven for 15 minutes, or until tender.

Cool and set aside.

Ingredients/Tempura-Fried Enoki

2 (2-oz) packages enoki mushrooms

1 egg

1 cup ice water

1/4 cup soy sauce

2-1/4 cups all-purpose flour, divided

2 qts canola oil

Method/Tempura-Fried Enoki

Beat the egg in a bowl, then add ice water and soy sauce.

Sift 1-1/4 cups flour into the bowl and mix lightly. Be careful not to overmix this batter.

Cut the bottoms off the mushrooms and split into 5 bunches.

Flour the mushrooms and dip into the batter.

Fry lightly in hot oil until outside is golden brown, then drain on paper towels.

Assembly

Assemble skewers in this order: yellow tomato, red tomato, radish piece, and Enoki mushroom as the base.

Chef Notes
The vegetables can all be marinated up to a couple of days in advance—and the longer they marinate, the better the flavor.

Variations
Pearl onions can be used instead of the radishes, adding texture as well as a sweeter flavor profile.

Makes about 20 servings

Grilled Enoki Mushrooms with Tomato Gelée and Radish Sprouts

Ingredients/Radish Sprouts

1 3 1/2-oz package fresh radish sprouts

Ingredients/Grilled Enoki Mushrooms

2 3-1/2-oz packages fresh enoki mushrooms

2 tsp olive oil

2 garlic cloves, chopped

2 stalks fresh rosemary leaves, finely chopped

kosher salt

white pepper

Method/Grilled Enoki Mushrooms

Mix the rosemary, garlic and olive oil; brush the mushrooms with this mixture.

Lightly grill the mushrooms over an open flame; season with salt and pepper while grilling.

Remove the mushrooms from the grill, chill and set aside.

Ingredients/Tomato Gelée

1-1/4 cup tomato water or tomato juice

3 gelatin sheets

1 cup cold water

Method/Tomato Gelée

Soak the gelatin sheets in the cold water until soft, then drain.

Put about 1/3 of the tomato water in a small pan with the softened gelatin. Stir over low heat until the gelatin is completely dissolved, then add the rest of the tomato water.

Remove the pan from heat. Pour the gelée into small spoons; chill in the refrigerator until soft set, about 30-45 minutes.

Assembly

Remove the spoons from the refrigerator.

Cut the bottoms off the enoki mushrooms, leaving 2-inch pieces. Place these enoki tips on top of the gelée in each spoon.

Top with fresh radish sprouts.

Chef Notes

For a stronger flavor, you can use tomato juice or Bloody Mary mix instead of tomato water when making the gelée.

Variations

Change the flavor profile and color by using flavored juices such as carrot, beet or spinach when making the gelée. The options are limitless with this fun and flavorful item.

Chef Notes
Enoki mushrooms soak up liquids quickly, so don't let them marinate too long or they will get too soft.

Variations
You can substitute shiitake or maitake mushrooms for the enoki, which will give you a more earthy flavor profile.

VEGETABLE INNOVATIONS

Watermelon Radish with Soy Scallion-Marinated Tomatoes and Marinated Enoki Mushrooms

Ingredients/Watermelon Radish

1 watermelon radish
4 tsp sesame oil
4 tsp rice wine vinegar
1 tsp black sesame seeds
1/2 tsp Thai chili powder

Method/Watermelon Radish

Peel the radish, then cut it in half and slice it into eighths, then julienne into matchstick-size pieces.

Toss the radish pieces with other ingredients in a bowl, then marinate for 1 hour.

Drain and set aside.

Ingredients/Marinated Enoki Mushrooms

2 (2-oz) packages enoki mushrooms
1/2 bunch scallions, chopped
1/4 bunch mint leaves, chopped
1/4 bunch cilantro leaves, chopped
4 tsp mirin
2 tsp grated fresh ginger
2 tsp sesame oil

Method/Marinated Enoki Mushrooms

Trim off the bottoms of the mushrooms.

Toss all the ingredients together and let marinate for no more than 10 minutes, then drain and set mushrooms aside.

Ingredients/Marinated Tomatoes

80 very small heirloom cherry tomatoes
1/2 bunch scallions, finely chopped on a slight bias
2 garlic cloves chopped
3 tsp soy sauce
1 tsp sesame oil

Method/Marinated Tomatoes

Toss the tomatoes with the other ingredients and let marinate for at least 1-2 hours.

Ingredients/Parsley

1/4 bunch Italian flat parsley
kosher salt

Method/Parsley

Remove the stems from the parsley. Deepfry the parsley until crispy.

Season with salt.

Assembly

Stand the mushrooms in 10 service cups or glasses. Add 8 pieces of marinated tomatoes to each.

Top with radish mixture and garnish with the fried parsley.

Vegetable INNOVATIONS

RADISH ◆ ENOKI MUSHROOMS ◆ TOMATO

EGGPLANT ◆ GARLIC ◆ RICOTTA

POTATO ◆ MUSHROOM ◆ ONION

BEETS ◆ GOAT CHEESE ◆ BALSAMIC VINEGAR

Stick

Spoon

Glass

Grilled Eggplant
with Garlic Roasted
Tomatoes and
Ricotta Salata

Crispy Eggplant
Discs with Garlic
Marinated Asparagus
and Ricotta Mousse

Eggplant Purée with
Garlic Chips and
Basil Ricotta

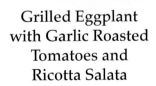

124

126

128

VEGETABLE INNOVATIONS

Makes about 20 servings

Grilled Eggplant with Garlic Roasted Tomatoes and Ricotta Salata

Ingredients/Grilled Eggplant

1 Japanese eggplant

1/4 bunch Italian parsley, chopped

3 garlic cloves finely chopped

kosher salt

white pepper

3 tsp olive oil

Method/Grilled Eggplant

Using a slicing machine, slice the eggplant lengthwise in 1/4-inch slices. Drizzle the slices with oil and season with salt and pepper. Sprinkle eggplant slices with parsley and chopped garlic.

On an open flame grill, grill the eggplant on both sides until tender, 4-5 minutes.

Chill and set aside.

Ingredients/Garlic Roasted Tomatoes

2 plum tomatoes

2 garlic cloves, chopped

2 tsp olive oil

1 stalk fresh rosemary leaves, chopped

Method/Garlic Roasted Tomatoes

Core each plum tomato and cut into 5 pieces. Toss with garlic, olive oil and rosemary.

Roast tomatoes in 350° oven for 15 minutes, until just tender.

Remove from oven and cool. Set aside.

Ingredients/Ricotta Salata

10 oz ricotta salata

2 garlic cloves, chopped

2 tsp olive oil

1 stalk fresh rosemary leaves, chopped

2 tsp balsamic vinegar

Method/Ricotta Salata

Cut ricotta into 20 pieces.

Combine balsamic and olive oil with garlic and rosemary and marinate ricotta in the mixture.

Set aside.

Ingredients/Basil Garlic Aioli

1/4 bunch fresh basil leaves, chopped

2 garlic cloves chopped

1/4 cup mayonnaise

1 tsp lemon juice

Method/Basil Garlic Aioli

Combine all ingredients in a bowl and mix with a whisk. Hold in refrigerator until ready to use.

Assembly

Lay one piece of eggplant on the worktable and cut in half vertically. At the end of each eggplant strip, lay a piece of tomato and a piece of ricotta next to each other, then roll up the eggplant like a cigar.

Top with Basil Garlic Aioli and skewer just before service.

Chef Notes
You can make the components of this item up to a day ahead of time and keep refrigerated without affecting the quality of the finished dish.

Variations
You can use zucchini or yellow squash instead of eggplant and mozzarella can be used instead of ricotta salata. While the textures are both firm, fresh mozzarella is a less acidic cheese and somewhat softer in texture.

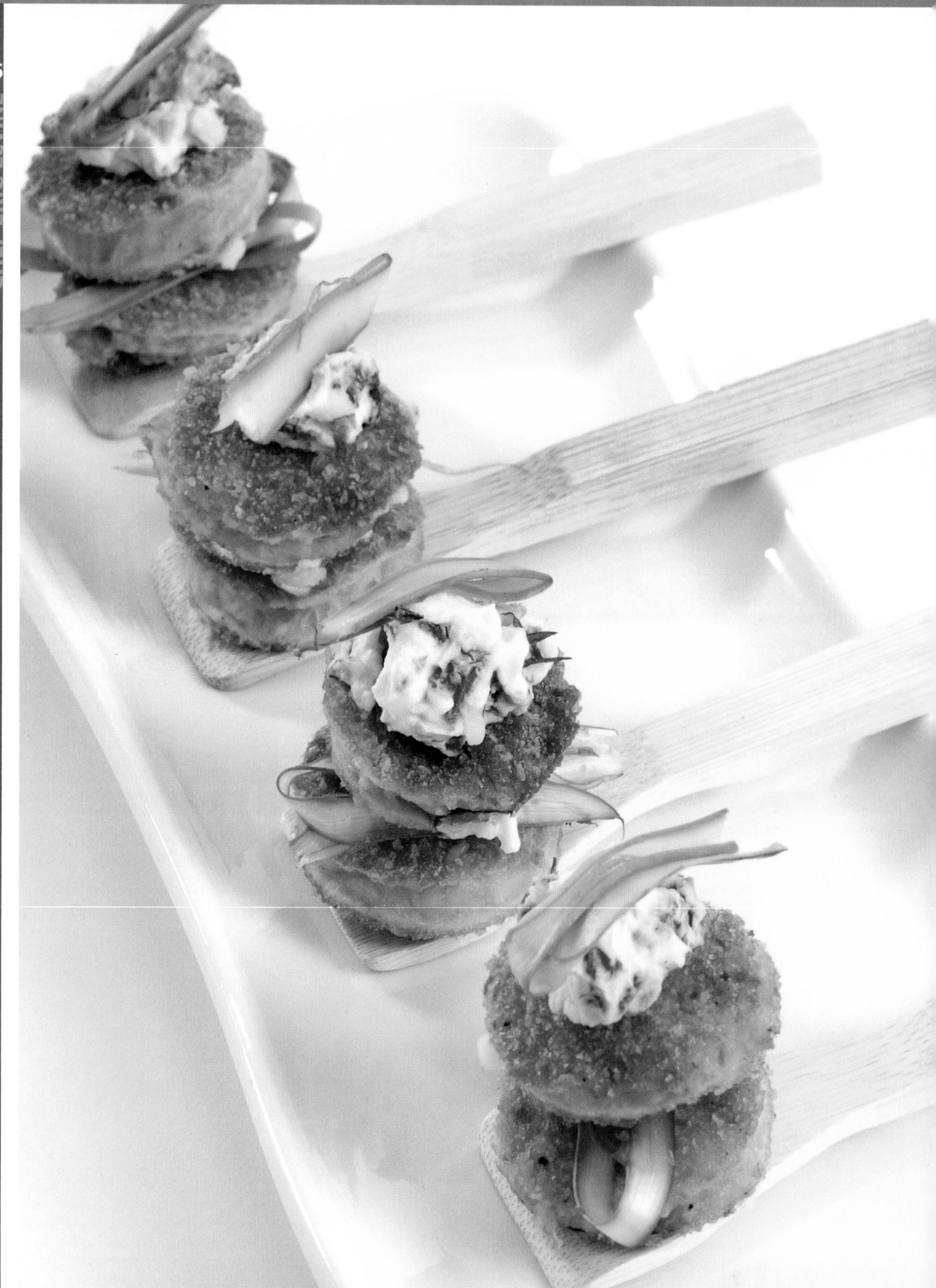

Crispy Eggplant Discs with Garlic Marinated Asparagus and Ricotta Mousse

Ingredients/Crispy Eggplant

1 Japanese eggplant

2 cups panko breadcrumbs

1 cup instant (Wondra) flour

1 cup egg wash (3 eggs and 1/4 cup water, whisked together)

kosher salt

white pepper

Method/Crispy Eggplant

Slice the eggplant, unpeeled, 1/4-inch circles; cut each slice in half to create half-moon shapes. Season with salt and pepper.

Dredge the eggplant slices in flour, then egg wash, then the breadcrumbs.

Deep-fry the eggplant slices until crispy, about 3 minutes, then remove from the fryer and season.

Hold warm until service for up to 30 minutes.

Ingredients/Garlic Asparagus

1 bunch thin asparagus

3 garlic cloves, chopped

8 tsp balsamic vinegar

6 tsp olive oil

1/4 bunch rosemary leaves, chopped

Method/Garlic Asparagus

Shave the asparagus into thin pieces with a peeler. Add the garlic and rosemary, then toss with the olive oil and balsamic vinegar and set aside.

Ingredients/Ricotta Mousse

1 cup ricotta cheese

1/4 bunch fresh basil leaves, chopped

1/2 cup sundried tomatoes, finely chopped

1/4 cup white balsamic vinegar

kosher salt

white pepper

Method/Ricotta Mousse

Mix all the ingredients in the bowl of a stand mixer, using the whisk attachment on high speed for 3 minutes, or until the mixture is light and fluffy.

Place the mousse in a piping bag and set aside.

Assembly

Place 1 piece of Crispy Eggplant in each spoon and top with 1/2 oz mousse and a strip of asparagus, then repeat layers.

Chef Notes
Drain the asparagus well.

Don't set the item up too early or the acid from the asparagus could cause the mousse to separate.

Variations
For more flavor, add a balsamic reduction or red wine reduction to the ricotta mix. Pesto will give a light herb-basil flavor, and add a vibrant green color.

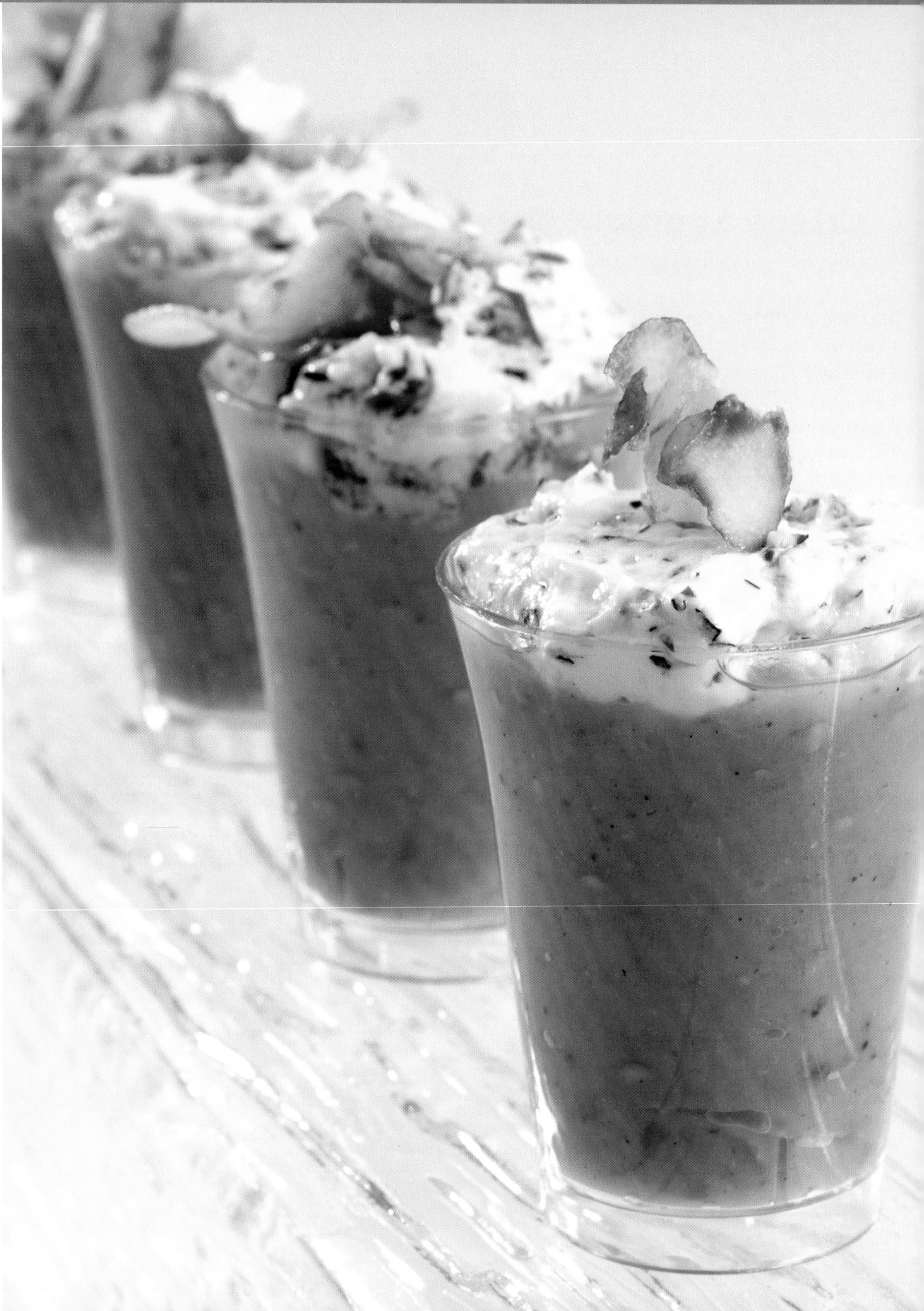

Makes about 10 servings

Eggplant Purée with Garlic Chips and Basil Ricotta

Ingredients/Eggplant Purée

1 eggplant
4 tsp olive oil
kosher salt
white pepper
3 tsp chopped garlic
2 sprigs rosemary leaves, chopped

Method/Eggplant Purée

Split the eggplant in half and score the flesh in a crisscross pattern. Toss both eggplant halves with the oil, salt and pepper.

Put the eggplant halves flesh side down on a roasting pan and roast at 325° for 25 minutes, until eggplant is tender.

Remove the eggplant halves from the oven and scoop the flesh into a food processor. Purée the eggplant flesh and add the garlic and rosemary leaves.

Season with salt and pepper to taste.

Ingredients/Garlic Chips

3 garlic cloves
1 qt frying oil
kosher salt

Method/Garlic Chips

Shave the garlic into very thin slices.

Fry the garlic slices in 300° oil until light brown and crispy.

Season with salt; set aside.

Ingredients/Basil Ricotta

2 cups ricotta cheese
1/4 bunch fresh basil leaves, chopped
kosher salt
white pepper
1/2 fresh red pepper, finely diced

Method

Mix the diced red pepper into the ricotta, then fold in the chopped basil. Season with salt and pepper and set aside.

Assembly

Spoon eggplant purée into the bottom of each service cup or glass. Spoon a little ricotta on top. Garnish with garlic chips.

Chef Notes

Use a sharp knife or razor when slicing the garlic.

Garlic begins to lose flavor as soon as it's cut, so slice it just before you're ready to fry it.

Variations

Use yellow squash or zucchini instead of eggplant; it's a great was to use the center of both squash when you're using the shells for other menu items. Zucchini centers can be mixed with tomato, onions and peppers for a ratatouille purée.

Vegetable INNOVATIONS

RADISH ◆ ENOKI MUSHROOMS ◆ TOMATO
EGGPLANT ◆ GARLIC ◆ RICOTTA

POTATO ◆ MUSHROOM ◆ ONION

BEETS ◆ GOAT CHEESE ◆ BALSAMIC VINEGAR

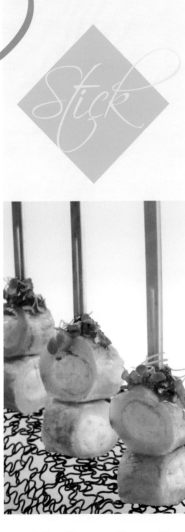

Stick

Spoon

Glass

Idaho Potato Cannoli
with Red Onion
Marmalade and
Porcini Dust

Potato Purée
with Caramelized
Onions and Crispy
Portobello Strips

Yukon Gold Potato
Salad with Scallions
and Mushroom Duxelle

132

134

136

Idaho Potato Cannoli with Red Onion Marmalade and Porcini Dust

Makes about 20 servings

Ingredients/Potato Cannoli

2 size 40 Idaho potatoes

1 cup heavy cream

1/2 lb butter

kosher salt

white pepper

Method/Potato Cannoli

Peel one potato and cut it into large pieces. Cover the pieces with water in a pot and cook until tender, about 20-25 minutes, then strain and return to pot over heat. Add the cream and 1/4 lb butter and mash until creamy. Season with salt and pepper. Put in refrigerator until ready to use.

Slice the second potato into 20 paper-thin slices.

Put the mashed potatoes in a piping bag and lay the potato slices out on a worktable.

Pipe mashed potatoes on each potato slice and then roll, seasoning with salt and pepper as you roll. (The starch in the potato slice will help seal the roll, creating a cylinder with the mashed potato in the center.) Melt the remaining 1/4 lb butter and brush on rolled potatoes.

Bake the rolled potatoes in a 350° oven for about 20-25 minutes, until outside is crispy and golden brown.

Ingredients/Red Onion Marmalade

1 red onion, medium dice

1/2 cup honey

1 tsp red pepper flakes

Method/Red Onion Marmalade

Combine the honey, onion and red pepper flakes in a saucepan. Bring to a boil and simmer for 10 minutes, or until the mixture is reduced and thickened to a marmalade texture.

Remove from the heat and chill until ready to serve.

Ingredients/Porcini Dust

4 lbs porcini mushrooms

Method/Porcini Dust

Slice the mushrooms and put in a dehydrator for 14 hours or until all the moisture is gone and the mushrooms are dry and brittle.

Process the dried mushrooms in a food processor until they have become dust. Set aside.

Assembly

Dust the edges of the Potato Cannoli with Porcini Dust, then slice each one in half (you will have 40 pieces). Skewer 2 halves of cannoli and top with Red Onion Marmalade.

Chef Notes

Dried porcini mushrooms are available at gourmet supply shops, if you don't have a dehydrator or just want to save time.

Variations

Try sweet potatoes, instead of Idaho potatoes for the "cannoli."

Creamygorg™ or blue cheese from BelGioioso Cheese can be added to the mashed potato filling for a different consistency and flavor.

Makes about 20 servings

Potato Purée with Caramelized Onions and Crispy Portobello Strips

Ingredients/Potato Purée

1 size 40 sweet potato, peeled and cut into chunks

1 size 40 Idaho potato, peeled and cut into chunks

1 cup heavy cream

1/2 lb butter

kosher salt

white pepper

Method/Potato Purée

Put potato chunks in two separate pots and cover with water. Bring both pots to a boil and cook until potatoes are tender, about 20-25 minutes. Drain and keep potatoes separate.

Add 1/2 cup cream to each pan of potatoes. Cook over low heat and mash until smooth with no lumps.

Put 1/4 lb butter in each pot and mix in. Season with salt and pepper.

Hold both pots of mashed potatoes until service. (You will need a pastry bag with a star tip for service.)

Ingredients/Caramelized Onions

1 red onion, julienned

2 tsp olive oil

1/4 bunch Italian flat parsley, chopped

kosher salt

white pepper

Method/Caramelized Onions

Heat the oil in a large sauté pan; add onions and caramelize until golden brown, about 5-6 minutes. Season onions with salt and pepper, add parsley, then remove from the heat and cool.

Ingredients/Crispy Portobello Strips

1 large portobello mushroom cap

1 cup milk

4 tsp cornstarch

kosher salt

white pepper

2 qts oil for frying

Method/Crispy Portobello Strips

Clean out the "feathers" from the mushroom cap. Cut the cap in half, then slice into thin strips.

Dredge the mushroom strips in the milk; drain slightly, then dredge in the cornstarch until coated.

Heat the oil in a deep fryer to 320° and fry mushroom strips until crispy. Remove from fryer and drain on paper towels, then season with salt and pepper.

Assembly

Place the mashed sweet potatoes and the mashed Idaho potatoes into a piping bag, side by side. Using a star tip, pipe the two potatoes onto each spoon.

Spoon Caramelized Onions on top of the potatoes and finish with Crispy Portobello Strips.

Chef Notes
Be sure to purée both potatoes until the texture is very smooth; you want to prevent lumps in the tip of the pastry bag.

Variations
Use purple potatoes for a variation in color, or mix puréed sautéed spinach into the mashed potatoes.

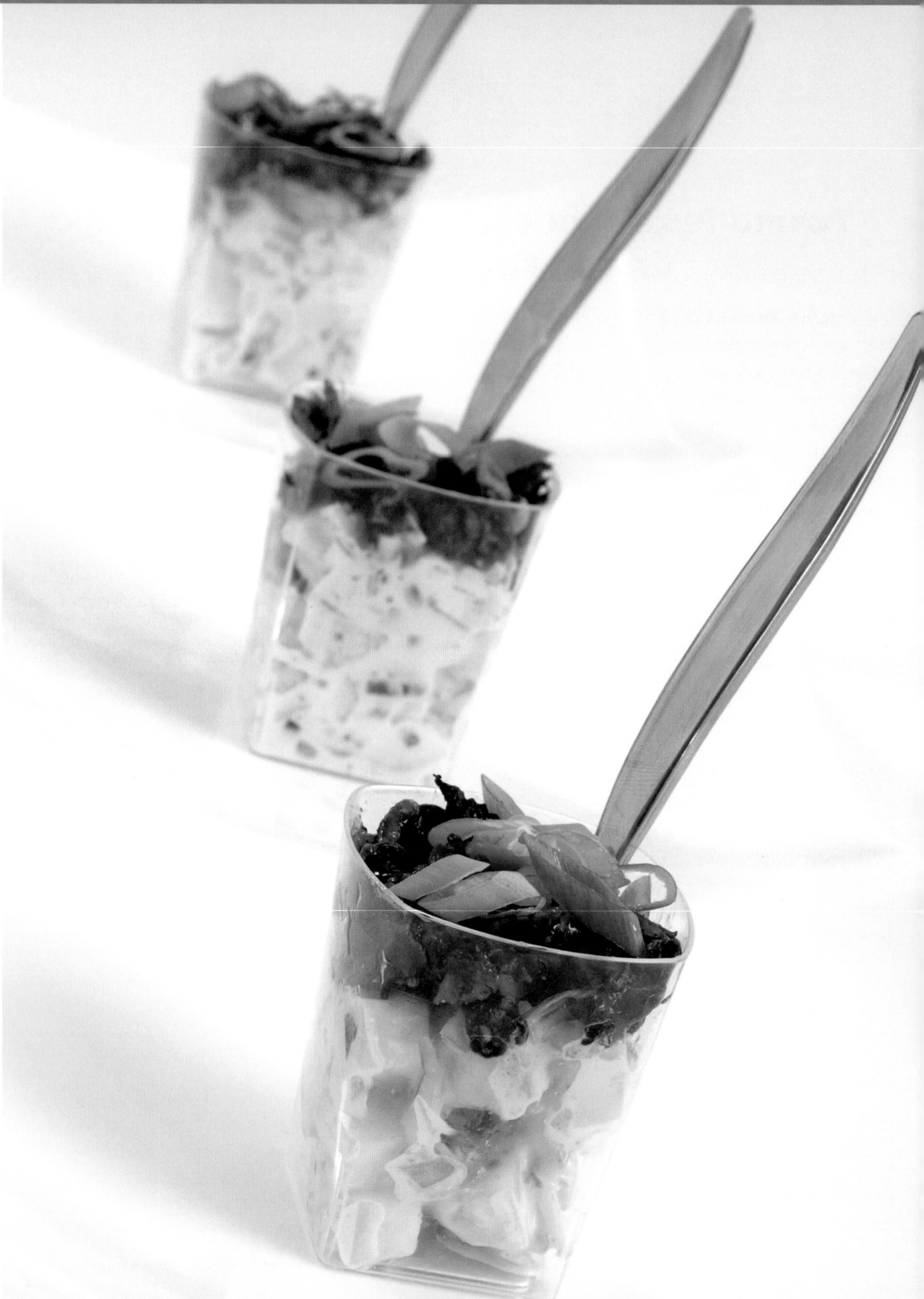

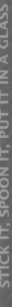

Makes about 20 servings

Yukon Gold Potato Salad with Scallions and Mushroom Duxelle

Ingredients/Yukon Gold Potato Salad

10 Yukon Gold potatoes

1/2 bunch scallions, sliced

1 stalk celery, finely chopped

1/4 red onion, finely chopped

1 tsp mustard

1 tsp mayonnaise

1 tsp Champagne vinegar

1 tsp paprika

kosher salt

white pepper

2 scallions

Method/Yukon Gold Potato Salad

Put the unpeeled potatoes in a pot and cover with water. Bring to a boil and cook until potatoes are fork-tender, about 20-25 minutes. Remove the potatoes from the water and cool on a sheet pan.

Combine the rest of the ingredients, except the 2 scallions, until thoroughly mixed.

Slice cooled potatoes into discs and toss lightly in the dressing mixture.

Let marinate for at least 2 hours.

Slice the 2 remaining scallions on the bias and reserve for garnish.

Ingredients/Mushroom Duxelle

3 Tbsp olive oil

1 lb cremini mushrooms, cleaned, stemmed and chopped

1/4 cup shallots, chopped

3 garlic cloves, chopped

1 cup port wine

kosher salt

black pepper

Method/Mushroom Duxelle

Heat the olive oil in a large sauté pan. When the oil is hot, add the mushrooms and sauté for 6 minutes.

Add the shallots and garlic and continue to sauté for 4 more minutes. Season with salt and pepper.

Add the port wine and cook until almost all the liquid has cooked off, 4–6 minutes. Remove the duxelle from the pan and cool completely.

Assembly

Divide potato salad among 20 service cups or glasses. Top each with 1 tsp Mushroom Duxelle, then finish with sliced scallions.

Add a fork to the service vessel just before serving.

Chef Notes
Make the potato salad and the duxelle at least a day before service to enhance the flavors.

Variations
Use Peruvian purple potatoes or banana potatoes for interesting color. Experiment with flavored mustards or aioli in the potato salad.

Vegetable INNOVATIONS

RADISH ◆ ENOKI MUSHROOMS ◆ TOMATO

EGGPLANT ◆ GARLIC ◆ RICOTTA

POTATO ◆ MUSHROOM ◆ ONION

BEETS ◆ GOAT CHEESE ◆ BALSAMIC VINEGAR

Stick

Spoon

Glass

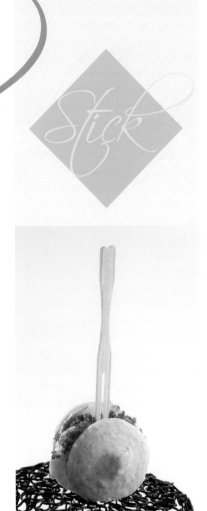

Beet Meringues with
Goat Cheese and
Balsamic Dust

Oven Roasted Beets
with Goat Cheese
Mousse and Balsamic
Reduction

Diced Red and Golden
Beets with Goat Cheese
Panna Cotta and
Balsamic Pearls

140

142

144

Chef Notes

Meringues can be made ahead of time, but they must be kept in a cool, dry place until service.

Variations

Both the meringue and the goat cheese mixture can easily be changed for interesting variations. For example, add carrot puree to the goat cheese and the meringues for new color and flavor.

Beet Meringues with Goat Cheese and Balsamic Dust

Ingredients/Beet Meringues

6 organic egg whites, at room temperature

1 cup maple syrup

1 small beet, peeled and minced

1 Tbsp vanilla extract

1/8 tsp cream of tartar or arrowroot

pinch of sea salt

Method/Beet Meringues

Put the minced beet and maple syrup in a small, heavy-bottomed saucepan and cook, covered, over medium-low heat for 30 minutes, until beets are cooked and soft. Strain the liquid and let cool. Save the chopped beets to use in another recipe.

Preheat the oven to 200° and line 3 baking sheets with parchment paper.

Splash a bit of white vinegar and salt in the bowl of a standing mixer and rub the bowl with a paper towel, then wipe clean. This ensures it is grease-free so egg whites will whip properly.

Beat the egg whites on medium-high until foamy and bubbly, then add sea salt and cream of tartar or arrowroot.

Increase the speed to high and keep beating until mixture is thick and creamy. Slowly add cooled maple syrup mixture and vanilla; mix until combined.

Put the mixture in a pastry bag and pipe into 40 shell shapes on the parchment-lined baking sheets.

Bake the shells at 200° for 1 hour, then turn off the oven but keep the door shut for at least 2–3 hours, until the meringues are crisp to the touch.

Ingredients/Goat Cheese Mousse

1/2 cup balsamic vinegar

1/4 cup honey

12 oz goat cheese

1/2 bunch chives, chopped

Method/Goat Cheese Mousse

Combine the balsamic vinegar and honey, bring to a boil then reduce heat and cook until it thickens, about 15-20 minutes. Remove from heat and cool. Reserve half for service, half for dust

Combine the goat cheese, chives and half the balsamic reduction in the bowl of a stand mixer and beat at medium speed with the whip attachment. Once the ingredients have been thoroughly mixed, turn the mixer to high speed and whip until smooth in appearance, about 4-5 minutes.

Put the mousse in a pastry bag and refrigerate until it has firmed up.

Ingredients/Balsamic Dust

1/4 cup balsamic reduction

80 g maltodextrin

Method/Balsamic Dust

Combine the balsamic reduction and maltodextrin in a food processor and mix until well combined. Pass through a China cap or fine mesh strainer to remove lumps.

Set aside in a cool, dry place.

Assembly

Place the meringues in two rows of 20 each.

Pipe Goat Cheese Mousse on one meringue, then top with another meringue, like a sandwich. Skewer the meringues and mousse and dust the edge with the Balsamic Dust.

Makes about 20 servings

Oven Roasted Beets with Goat Cheese Mousse and Balsamic Reduction

Ingredients/Oven Roasted Beets

2 red beets

2 tsp balsamic vinegar

2 tsp olive oil

kosher salt

pepper

1 sprig fresh rosemary leaves, chopped

Method/Oven Roasted Beets

Peel and cut beets into 20 1/2-inch wedges.

Toss all ingredients together and season with salt and pepper. Place beets on a sheet pan and bake at 325° for 25 minutes or until tender.

Cool and set aside.

Ingredients/Goat Cheese Mousse

12 oz goat cheese

4 garlic cloves

2 tsp olive oil

1/2 bunch fresh thyme, chopped

kosher salt

white pepper

Method/Goat Cheese Mousse

Toss garlic cloves with the olive oil, salt and pepper. Roast at 350° for 15 minutes, until tender.

Mash the garlic in a mixing bowl while still hot, then add the goat cheese and chopped thyme and mix well.

Put mousse in a piping bag; set aside.

Ingredients/Balsamic Reduction

1 cup balsamic vinegar

1/2 cup honey

3 tsp cornstarch

2 tsp water

Method/Balsamic Reduction

Combine the honey and vinegar in a pot. Cook until reduced by half, about 8-10 minutes.

Add cornstarch to water and create a slurry. Add to the honey and vinegar a little at a time, until the thickness is like honey.

Assembly

Pipe the goat cheese mousse into spoons. Top each with 3 pieces of roasted beets.

Spoon a little Balsamic Reduction over the beets.

Garnish with fresh thyme.

Chef Notes
Using several different kinds of beets can enhance the presentation by adding color.

Variations
Use different cheeses—blue cheese, port salut or a soft boursin—to make the mousse, for a variety of flavor profiles.

Diced Red and Golden Beets with Goat Cheese Panna Cotta and Balsamic Pearls

Ingredients/Beets

1 red beet

1 golden beet

salt and pepper

4 tsp white balsamic vinegar

1/4 bunch chervil, chopped

Method/Beets

Peel and dice both beets, keeping separated.

Lightly blanch beets in boiling water until tender, about 3 minutes, then chill in an ice bath and set aside.

Right before service, toss the beets with the white balsamic, chervil, salt and pepper.

Ingredients/Goat Cheese Panna Cotta

3 cups cream

1 cup goat's milk

1 envelope powdered gelatin, bloomed in 3 Tbsp water

7 oz goat cheese

Method/Goat Cheese Panna Cotta

Gently heat the cream and milk in a saucepan. When it's hot, whisk in the gelatin and water mixture.

Whisk in the goat cheese until the mixture is smooth; pour into 10 4-oz service cups.

Chill in the refrigerator for at least 4 hours, preferably 12.

Ingredients/Balsamic Pearls

2 gm sodium alginate

150 ml balsamic vinegar

2 gm calcium chloride

400 ml water

Method/Balsamic Pearls

Combine the sodium alginate and balsamic vinegar and blend.

Combine the calcium chloride and half of the water in a small bowl. Pour the rest of the water into a separate bowl to finish the pearls.

Put the balsamic mixture into the reservoir of a pearl dropper and pull into the dispenser tips with the plunger. Slowly dispense the balsamic solution over the calcium chloride solution to form pearls.

Let the pearls remain in the solution for 30 seconds; remove with a small strainer, then drop into cold water to remove any calcium chloride flavor. Remove from water and store in a plastic container in the refrigerator.

Assembly

Put a layer of golden beets into serving cups or glasses until about 1/3 filled. Pipe in just enough mousse to cover the beets, then spoon in a layer of red beets. Top with more mousse.

Drizzle 1/4 tsp of balsamic reduction on top of mousse. Add 1/2 tsp of Balsamic Pearls and garnish with thyme or micro greens.

Chef Notes

Pat dry the beets well to keep them from bleeding in to the mousse.

You can make the pearls ahead of time and store in balsamic reduction until needed. Drain in small strainer before using.

Variations

Use tomatoes instead of beets for a subtle but interesting change of flavor. You can use tomatillos, vine-ripened tomatoes or beefsteak tomatoes. Marinate the tomatoes you choose in salt, pepper, olive oil, garlic and rosemary and then roast until tender, 4–6 minutes.

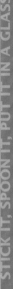

CHAPTER FIVE

PRESENTATIONS

BLUE CHEESE ◆ BACON ◆ ONION
PEPATO CHEESE ◆ SPINACH ◆ BUTTERNUT SQUASH
PARMESAN ◆ BASIL ◆ ONION
MOZZARELLA ◆ OLIVES ◆ ONION

Guests love cheese, whether it's simple wedges, slices and cubes on a buffet or something truly elegant. With cheese as the main ingredient, hors d'oeuvre can be exciting and interesting—and yet cost-effective for both the caterer and the client.

These recipes show that while cheese may be expected, the presentation doesn't have to be. Cheese is combined with an array of interesting vegetables, herbs and even a little meat to create unique and satisfying tastes.

Cheese PRESENTATIONS

BLUE CHEESE ◆ BACON ◆ ONION
PEPATO CHEESE ◆ SPINACH ◆ BUTTERNUT SQUASH
PARMESAN ◆ BASIL ◆ ONION
MOZZARELLA ◆ OLIVES ◆ ONION

Gorgonzola, Bacon and
Chive Lollipops

Blue Cheese Ravioli
with Pancetta Crisps
and Red Onion Confit

Blue Cheese and Bacon
Custard with Brown
Sugar Bacon Crisp and
Crispy Onions

150   152   154

Blue Cheese, Bacon, Onion

Makes about 20 servings

Gorgonzola, Bacon and Chive Lollipops

Ingredients/Lollipops

1 lb gorgonzola, crumbled

6 strips smoked bacon

1 bunch fresh chives, finely chopped

20 sticks

Method/Lollipops

Cook bacon until golden brown, finely chop and set aside. Pour grease into a cup and reserve for Bacon Dust.

In a medium bowl, mix the gorgonzola and bacon pieces and mix thoroughly.

Add half the chopped chives to the cheese mixture and mix thoroughly; reserve the other half of the chive for garnish.

Refrigerate the mixture, covered for at least 2 hours, then roll into 20 balls. Refrigerate the cheese balls so they will be firm.

Ingredients/Bacon Dust

4 oz bacon drippings

1/2 cup maltodextrin

Method/Bacon Dust

Put the bacon drippings in a food processor and begin to process. Slowly add the maltodextrin to create dust.

Pass the dust through a fine China cap or tamis to remove lumps. Set aside.

Ingredients/Chive Mist

1 bunch chives

1/2 cup chicken stock

2 misting bottles

Method/Chive Mist

Puree the chives and stock in a blender until smooth. Strain through a fine China cap to get out any lumps that would clog a mister.

Assembly

Roll the gorgonzola balls in the remaining chopped chives. Put sticks into the cheese balls.

Put the Bacon Dust in a shallow pan. Lightly tap each cheese ball in the Bacon Dust until the bottom is coated.

Put more Bacon Dust on each service plate and place each lollipop on the dust.

Place the mist bottle on the tray as the lollipops are passed and have each guest mist a lollipop before eating it.

Chef Notes

Don't refrigerate the Bacon Dust;
moisture will soften and liquefy it.

Variations

Other soft cheeses, like Port Salut or goat cheese,
make a milder, subtly different hors d'oeuvre.

Chef Notes

The ravioli can be made up to 1 day ahead and heated on-site just before service.

Variations

You can fill the ravioli with a wild mushroom or butternut squash mixture, instead of the blue cheese mixture, and then change to a complementary foam flavor, such as garlic-rosemary for the wild mushrooms or cinnamon-brown sugar for the butternut squash.

CHEESE PRESENTATIONS

Spoon

Makes about 20 servings

Blue Cheese Ravioli with Pancetta Crisps and Red Onion Confit

Ingredients/Blue Cheese Ravioli

8 oz Creamygorg™ (soft gorgonzola cheese)

1 cup ricotta cheese

20 4x4-inch wonton skins

egg wash (1 egg beated with 1 Tbsp cold water)

2 shallots, chopped

2 oz Italian parsley, chopped

3 oz pancetta in small dice

1 qt chicken stock

Method/Blue Cheese Ravioli

Add pancetta to a heated sauté pan. When the pancetta starts to brown, add the shallots and sauté for about 6-7 minutes. Remove pancetta and shallots from heat and cool in refrigerator.

Combine gorgonzola and ricotta cheese and add cooled pancetta and shallots. Fold together until thoroughly mixed, then put in a piping bag.

Lay out wonton skins, one at a time. Cut each into four squares. Brush the edges with egg wash.

Pipe 1/2 tsp of the filling into the center of each wonton. Fold from one corner, to form a triangle, and press the edges together to seal. With a pasta wheel, trim the excess.

Fill a 4-qt pot with water and bring to a boil. Put the ravioli in the boiling water and cook fully, about 5–8 minutes, then shock the ravioli in ice water to stop cooking.

Toss ravioli in olive oil and set aside.

Ingredients/Pancetta Crunch

1 lb pancetta, diced in 1/4-inch cubes

1/4 bunch fresh basil leaves, chopped

Method/Pancetta Crunch

Sauté pancetta until it's crispy and fat is rendered. Put pancetta cubes on paper towels to drain, then toss lightly with the basil leaves.

Ingredients/Red Onion Confit

1 red onion, chopped

2 shallots, chopped

3 garlic cloves, chopped

1/2 bunch rosemary leaves, chopped

1/2 cup honey

1 tsp red pepper flakes

1 tsp oil

Method/Red Onion Confit

Sauté the garlic, red onion and shallots in oil. Add the rosemary, honey and red pepper flakes and lower heat; cook until mixture is thick, about 15 minutes.

Place mixture in a small bowl to cool.

Ingredients/Blue Cheese Foam

1/2 lb blue cheese, crumbled

2 cups heavy cream, chilled

kosher salt

white pepper

Method/Blue Cheese Foam

Pour the cream into a large saucepan and bring to a boil over medium-high heat. As soon as the cream boils, remove from the heat.

Add the blue cheese and use a handheld immersion blender to puree until smooth. (You could also transfer the cream and cheese to a food processor and process until smooth.) Strain into a large bowl through a chinois or fine-mesh sieve. Season with salt and pepper and set aside to cool at room temperature.

When cooled, pour the blue cheese mixture into the chilled canister of a foamer (this recipe should half fill a foamer). Charge the mixture with 1 or 2 charges. Chill for at least 2 hours before serving.

If you don't have a foamer, use just 1 cup of cream and whisk the ingredients together just before serving.

Assembly

Heat the prepared ravioli in chicken stock for about 10 minutes and place 2-3 on each spoon. Top with Pancetta Crunch, spoon on some Red Onion Confit and spray on Blue Cheese Foam to finish.

Makes about 10 servings

Blue Cheese and Bacon Custard with Brown Sugar Bacon Crisp and Crispy Onions

Ingredients/Blue Cheese Custard

1/2 cup Creamygorg™ (soft gorgonzola cheese)

3 large eggs

1-1/2 cups heavy cream

1/2 tsp kosher salt

1/4 tsp black pepper

1/2 cup bacon, cooked and diced

Method/Blue Cheese Custard

Mix the eggs, heavy cream, bacon, cheese, salt and pepper together until just combined (if the custard mix gets too much air in it, the custards will cook unevenly). Put into a silicone mold that makes 10 half-spheres (available online). Place mold in a roasting pan.

Pour enough boiling water into the roasting pan, around the mold, so that it creates a water bath for the custards. Cover the roasting pan tightly with foil and carefully place on the center shelf of a 300° oven. Bake for 30 minutes.

Check the custards by folding the foil back very carefully and gently jiggling the mold. If the custards are set, each will shake as a firm unit. If they are not done, waves of custard will shiver in the center. If the custards need to cook longer, re-cover and bake, checking every 5 minutes until done. Remove the pan from the oven and take the mold out of the water bath. Set aside.

Ingredients/Brown Sugar Bacon

10 pieces applewood-smoked bacon

1/2 cup brown sugar

Method/Brown Sugar Bacon

Line a sheet pan with parchment paper and lay the bacon slices on the paper.

Rub the brown sugar into the bacon, pressing it on.

Cook in a 350° oven until the bacon is crispy and the sugar has caramelized, about 8-10 minutes.

Let cool. Cut each bacon piece in half. Set aside 10 half pieces and crumble the rest.

Ingredients/Crispy Onions

1 red onion, peeled and shaved into fine rings

1 cup milk

2 cups instant (Wondra) flour

kosher salt

white pepper

Method/Crispy Onions

Soak the onions in the milk for 5 minutes, then drain and dredge in the flour.

Cook the onions in a fryer until golden brown. Remove from fryer and season.

Set aside.

Assembly

Put some crumbled bacon in the bottom of each service cup or glass. Put two half-spheres of Blue Cheese Custard on top of the bacon, to form a ball. Place a half piece of bacon next to the ball and top with Crispy Onions.

Chef Notes
Cooking time for custards can vary, so you need to watch carefully. Fresh eggs cook faster than older eggs.

Adding oven-roasted tomatoes to the custard will give it a lighter flavor.

Variations
Pancetta or prosciutto can be used instead of bacon for a somewhat saltier taste, which also will give the panna cotta a richer flavor.

Cheese
PRESENTATIONS

BLUE CHEESE ◆ BACON ◆ ONION

PEPATO CHEESE ◆ SPINACH ◆ BUTTERNUT SQUASH

PARMESAN ◆ BASIL ◆ ONION

MOZZARELLA ◆ OLIVES ◆ ONION

Stick

Spoon

Glass

Marinated Pepato with
Spinach Gelée and
Roast Butternut Squash

Pepato Cheese with
Sautéed Spinach and
Butternut Squash Purée

Pepato Bread Pudding
with Crispy Spinach
and Butternut Squash

158

160

162

Chef Notes
*Use powdered gelatin to control the thickness and
viscosity of the gelée squares best.*

Variations
*Chopped hazelnuts or pecans can be dusted around
the skewer to add texture and flavor.*

CHEESE PRESENTATIONS

Marinated Pepato with Spinach Gelée and Roast Butternut Squash

Ingredients/Marinated Pepato

1 lb pepato cheese, cut into 20 cubes

olive oil

1/2 bunch fresh basil leaves, chopped

2 garlic cloves, chopped

1/4 tsp red pepper flakes

kosher salt

white pepper

Method/Marinated Pepato

Toss cheese cubes with basil, garlic, oil, red pepper flakes, salt and pepper and let marinate. Refrigerate until ready to use.

Ingredients/Spinach Gelée

10 oz baby spinach

1/2 cup heavy cream

3 cloves garlic, chopped

2 tsp olive oil

1/2 red pepper, diced

kosher salt

white pepper

1/4 cup chicken stock

4 oz gelatin powder

Method/Spinach Gelée

Sauté the garlic in the olive oil, then add spinach. Cook until the spinach is wilted, about 3-5 minutes. Remove from the heat and purée in a blender.

Dilute the gelatin in the chicken stock and add half of the mixture to the blender with the spinach mixture. Continue to purée the mixture until it's smooth, then drain the liquid from the spinach through a China cap; discard the pulp of the spinach.

Heat the cream in a saucepan for about 6-8 minutes, season with salt and pepper, then add the rest of the gelatin and stock mixture.

Combine the cream mixture and the spinach mixture in a bowl. Add chopped red pepper and mix thoroughly.

Spoon the mixture into 1/2-inch square silicone forms and refrigerate.

Ingredients/Roast Butternut Squash

1 butternut squash, peeled and cut into ½-inch cubes

1/2 lb butter

1/4 bunch fresh sage leaves, chopped

kosher salt

white pepper

Method

Toss all ingredients together.

Roast the squash cubes in a 350° oven for 30 minutes, or until fork tender.

Cool and set aside.

Ingredients/Roasted Garlic Reduction

6 garlic cloves

3 tsp olive oil

1 cup plus 3 tsp balsamic vinegar

3 tsp honey

Method/Roasted Garlic Reduction

Toss the garlic with the oil and 3 tsp balsamic vinegar.

Roast the garlic in a 325° oven until it is golden brown and soft, about 10-12 minutes. Remove from oven, put in a blender and purée until smooth.

Add the honey and 1 cup of balsamic vinegar to the garlic purée, put in a pan over medium heat and reduce for about 10 minutes.

Cool and set aside.

Assembly

Pop the Spinach Gelée squares out of the silicone mold.

Put food on each skewer in this order: squash, gelée square, Marinated Pepato.

Drizzle Roasted Garlic Reduction on each skewer.

CHEF ERIC LeVINE

CHEESE PRESENTATIONS

Makes about 20 servings

Pepato Cheese with Sautéed Spinach and Butternut Squash Purée

Ingredients/Pepato Cheese

1 lb pepato cheese, finely grated

Method/Pepato Cheese

Line a sheet pan with parchment paper. Spoon cheese on the parchment paper by tablespoonfuls and form into circles.

Bake cheese circles in 350° oven for 9 minutes, or until the cheese circles are crisp. Remove from oven and let cool. Set aside.

Ingredients/Sautéed Spinach

10 oz baby spinach

1/2 cup heavy cream

3 cloves garlic, chopped

2 tsp olive oil

1/2 red pepper, diced

kosher salt

white pepper

Method/Sautéed Spinach

Sauté the garlic in oil; add the spinach and peppers and sauté, then add the cream and season with salt and pepper.

Keep hot until ready to serve.

Ingredients/Butternut Squash Purée

1 butternut squash, peeled and cut into chunks

1/2 lb butter, melted

1/4 bunch fresh sage leaves, chopped

kosher salt

white pepper

Method/Butternut Squash Purée

Toss the squash with the sage, butter, salt and pepper.

Roast in a 350° oven for 30 minutes or until fork-tender. Remove from oven and purée until smooth. Season with salt and pepper, if needed.

Ingredients/Chili Maple Glaze

3 tsp chili powder

3/4 cup maple syrup

3 oz balsamic vinegar

Method/Chili Maple Glaze

Combine all ingredients in a saucepan and bring to a simmer. Reduce until the mixture is thick like syrup, about 8-10 minutes.

Remove from heat and cool. Set aside.

Assembly

Put the squash mixture into a piping bag and pipe onto spoons.

Spoon spinach on top of the squash. Pipe on more purée.

Insert a pepato crisp into the purée on the spoon.

Drizzle a little Chili Maple Glaze on top.

Chef Notes
The cheese crisps can be made up to 2 days in advance, as long as they are held in a airtight container.

Variations
Salty bacon or pancetta, combined with a potato puree instead of the squash, works well with cheese crisps and Chili Maple Glaze.

Ingredients/Pepato Bread Pudding

2 Tbsp unsalted butter, at room temperature

12 slices good quality white sandwich bread, crusts trimmed off (about 8 oz total)

5 oz crumbled goat cheese or 6 oz crumbled feta cheese

1/2 lb sundried tomatoes, finely diced

6 eggs

2 cups milk

3 Tbsp prepared pesto

1/4 cup freshly grated pepato cheese

Method/Pepato Bread Pudding

Grease the bottom of a 9x13-inch baking dish or other shallow 3-quart baking pan.

Butter each bread slice on one side. Stack the bread, 6 at a time, and cut across the diagonal into triangles. Place half of the bread pieces, buttered sides down, in the bottom of the prepared dish. Scatter the cheese over the bread in one layer. Scatter the tomatoes over the cheese. Top with the remaining buttered bread pieces, buttered sides up.

Whisk the eggs, milk and pesto together in a bowl until well-blended, then pour over the bread and cheese mixture in the dish. Push the top pieces of bread down lightly with the back of a fork so they soak up some liquid. Sprinkle the grated pepato over the top. Let the pan sit in the refrigerator for 3 hours before baking.

Bake the pudding at 350° for 35 minutes with foil covering the pan, then remove the foil and continue to bake until pudding is puffed and golden brown on top, 25–30 more minutes.

Cool the bread pudding and hold in the refrigerator until the next day.

Using a round biscuit or cookie cutter, cut 2-inch circles from the pudding. Set aside at room temperature for up to 30 minutes.

Makes about 10 servings

Pepato Bread Pudding with Crispy Spinach and Butternut Squash

Ingredients/Crispy Spinach

10 baby spinach leaves

1 qt oil for frying

Method/Crispy Spinach

Heat the oil to 350°. Drop the leaves into the fryer until crisp. Remove from the oil and drain on paper towels. Set aside.

Ingredients/Roasted Butternut Squash

1 large butternut squash, peeled, seeded and diced into 1/4-inch cubes

1/4 cup olive oil

3 cloves garlic, minced

2 Tbsp fresh sage leaves, chopped

salt

freshly ground black pepper

Method/Roasted Butternut Squash

Line a baking sheet with parchment paper.

Toss the squash cubes with the oil, garlic, sage and salt and pepper. Spread in a single layer on the baking sheet.

Roast the squash in a 375° oven until the squash is tender in the center and the outside is brown and crisp, 25–30 minutes. Take out of the oven when done, put in a serving bowl and set aside.

Ingredients/Balsamic Mousse

1 cup balsamic vinegar

1/2 cup honey

3 tsp cornstarch

2 tsp water

1 cup heavy cream

Method/Balsamic Mousse

Combine the honey and vinegar in a pot. Cook until reduced by half.

Add the cornstarch to the water and create a slurry. Add this slurry to the honey and vinegar a little at a time, until it's the consistency of honey.

Whip the cream in a mixer on high until soft peaks form. Slowly drizzle 1/2 cup of the balsamic reduction into the whipped cream and whip until the mixture forms stiff peaks.

Place the mousse in a piping bag.

Assembly

Warm the bread pudding rounds in a 350° oven for 3 minutes.

Pipe butternut squash into the bottom of each service cup or glass. Put a round of bread pudding on top of the squash, then pipe balsamic mousse on top of the bread pudding. Top with Crispy Spinach pieces.

Chef Notes

Make the bread pudding a day ahead to allow flavors to develop. This will also make it easier to cut.

Variations

For a lighter dish, add roasted chicken pieces to the bread pudding. With the chicken, use arugula instead of spinach. Sauté the arugula with shallots and thyme, then finish with a touch of red wine.

Cheese
PRESENTATIONS

BLUE CHEESE ◆ BACON ◆ ONION
PEPATO CHEESE ◆ SPINACH ◆ BUTTERNUT SQUASH

PARMESAN ◆ BASIL ◆ ONION

MOZZARELLA ◆ OLIVES ◆ ONION

Stick

Spoon

Glass

Parmesan and Basil
Marshmallows with
Marinated Sundried
Tomatoes and
Basil Dust

166

Basil Panna Cotta with
Parmesan Mousse and
Marinated Tomatoes

168

Tomato Confit with
Micro Basil
Fennel Salad and
Parmesan Crisps

170

Parmesan, Basil, Onion

CHEF ERIC LeVINE

Chef Notes
The marshmallows can be made up to 3 days before use, as long as they are kept in an airtight container.

Variations
Instead of basil marshmallows, make garlic rosemary marshmallows.

Parmesan and Basil Marshmallows with Marinated Sundried Tomatoes and Basil Dust

Ingredients/Parmesan and Basil Marshmallows

1-2/3 cups milk

5 gm agar-agar

5-1/2 oz Parmesan

3-1/2 oz fresh basil, chopped

2 egg whites

kosher salt

white pepper

Method/Parmesan and Basil Marshmallows

Combine milk and agar-agar in a saucepan and stir to combine.

Add 3 1/2 oz Parmesan and turn on low heat under saucepan; bring liquid to a simmer, whisking continuously. Simmer for 5 minutes, then strain through a fine sieve into a cold bowl; cool until the liquid starts to thicken (5–7 minutes).

Whisk the egg whites and a pinch of salt in an electric mixer until soft peaks form. Fold the egg white mixture into the milk mixture. Season to taste.

Pour the mixture into a 4x8 tray lined with plastic wrap; refrigerate until set (2–3 hours).

Using a hot knife, cut the mixture into 1-1/2 inch squares. Roll the squares in the remaining Parmesan and store in refrigerator until needed.

Ingredients/Marinated Sundried Tomatoes

20 sundried tomatoes, quartered

2 garlic cloves, chopped

1/4 bunch fresh basil, chopped

1/2 cup balsamic vinegar

1/2 cup olive oil

kosher salt

white pepper

Method/Marinated Sundried Tomatoes

Combine all ingredients and marinate for 24 hours in refrigerator, then drain and set aside.

Ingredients/Basil Dust

1/4 bunch fresh basil, chopped

1/2 bunch fresh basil puréed with 1/2 cup oil, then strained

1 cup maltodextrin

kosher salt

white pepper

Method/Basil Dust

Combine fresh basil and basil oil and purée in blender. Let sit overnight.

Strain oil and put in food processor. Add maltodextrin and pulse until a dust is formed.

Pass the dust through a fine China cap to remove lumps. Set aside.

Assembly

Alternate two marshmallows and two pieces of sundried tomato on each skewer.

Sprinkle Basil Dust on the serving tray and place the skewers on top of the dust.

CHEF ERIC LeVINE

Chef Notes
All ingredients can be made up to 2 days ahead of time.

*Be careful to properly measure the quantity of gelatin.
If you use too much, the panna cotta
can be too firm and almost rubber-like.*

Variations:
*You can create a very different combination of
vegetables by making a rosemary panna cotta and
a roasted garlic panna cotta and then topped with
roasted eggplant and a balsamic mousse.*

Makes about 10 servings

Basil Panna Cotta with Parmesan Mousse and Marinated Tomatoes

Ingredients/Basil Panna Cotta

2 oz basil leaves, chopped

2 packets unflavored gelatin

1 qt heavy cream

kosher salt

white pepper

Method/Basil Panna Cotta

Dissolve the unflavored gelatin in the cold cream. Season with salt and pepper to taste. Put the cream in a heavy stainless steel saucepan and add the basil. Bring to a slow simmer, stirring frequently for 20 minutes.

Pour into a silicone mold with 1-oz round cups. Refrigerate for about 3 hours.

Ingredients/Parmesan Mousse

2 cups heavy cream

4 cloves garlic, crushed with the back of a flat knife

3 egg yolks

1 packet of gelatin, dissolved in 2 Tbsp cold water

1 cup Parmesan, grated

kosher salt

white pepper

2 Tbsp chopped basil

Method/Parmesan Mousse

Put the garlic cloves in 1 cup cream and simmer over medium-low heat in a small saucepan for 10 minutes.

Place the egg yolks in a small bowl and whisk in 1/3 cup of the warm cream. Add the egg mixture to the rest of the cream in the saucepan, whisking constantly. Continue to heat the cream over medium heat until thickened, about 8-10 minutes.

Stir the softened gelatin into the cream and egg mixture and continue stirring until the gelatin is dissolved. Add the Parmesan, salt and pepper and stir until the cheese is fully incorporated.

Remove the pan from the heat and set in a cool, not cold, water bath.

Whip the remaining cup of cream to stiff peaks.

When the custard is cool, but before it has started to set up, fold in the whipped cream and add the chopped basil. Season to taste and pour into a hotel pan.

Chill the custard for at least 3 hours; overnight is best.

Ingredients/Marinated Tomatoes

3 Tbsp fresh parsley leaves, chopped

1 Tbsp sugar

1-1/2 tsp garlic salt

1-1/2 tsp seasoned salt

1/2 tsp ground pepper

3/4 tsp chopped fresh thyme leaves

3/4 cup vegetable oil

1/2 cup red wine vinegar

3 scallions, chopped

20 cherry tomatoes

Method/Marinated Tomatoes

Combine all ingredients except tomatoes in a mixing bowl and whisk well.

Cut the cherry tomatoes in half and put in a resealable plastic bag. Pour the marinade over the tomatoes and seal the bag. Marinate at room temperature for up to 2 hours, turning the bag occasionally.

Assembly

Place Basil Panna Cotta in spoons. Put 2 tomato halves on top of the panna cotta, top with a dollop of mousse and garnish with basil microgreens.

Chef Notes
Mix the fennel salad just before assembling the cups,
to keep the micro greens and chervil from wilting.

Variations
Instead of the Tomato Confit, use portobello mushrooms
or bell peppers. Try celeriac instead of fennel in the salad.

CHEESE PRESENTATIONS

Makes about 10 servings

Tomato Confit with Micro Basil Fennel Salad and Parmesan Crisps

Ingredients/Tomato Confit

1 lb Roma tomatoes (about 5 medium tomatoes)

2 Tbsp olive oil

2 medium garlic cloves, halved

2 fresh thyme sprigs

1 medium dried bay leaf, crushed

1 tsp kosher salt

1/2 tsp granulated sugar

1/4 tsp freshly ground black pepper

Method/Tomato Confit

Slice 1/8 inch off the tops and bottoms of the tomatoes. Stand each tomato on one end and slice downward, following the curve and just cutting into the flesh, leaving behind the seeds (the pieces you cut off will resemble petals). Discard the seeds and pulpy portion.

Combine tomato petals with the remaining ingredients in a medium bowl and toss to coat. Spread the tomato petals, cut side down, on a baking sheet, spaced about 1/2 inch apart. Pour the remaining contents of the bowl over tomatoes.

Roast the tomatoes in a 325° oven until they're shriveled and dark red but still hold their shape, about 45–50 minutes. Cool in the pan, then transfer to a container with a tight-fitting lid and cover with any remaining oil from the baking sheet (add additional oil if there's not enough to cover the tomatoes). Store in the refrigerator until ready to use.

Ingredients/Tomato Leather

1/3 cup finely chopped onion

2 garlic cloves, chopped

1 Tbsp olive oil

1 tsp butter

12 oz tomato paste

1 tsp kosher salt

1 tsp sugar

2 tsp chopped parsley

2 tsp chopped fresh basil

1 tsp chopped fresh oregano

Method/Tomato Leather

Sauté the garlic, onion, parsley, basil and oregano in oil for 5–7 minutes. Add butter to cooked garlic mixture, then add tomato paste, salt and sugar and combine.

Remove the mixture from the heat and spread on a sheet pan covered with parchment paper.

Bake in a 140° oven for 6 hours; watch to make sure it doesn't burn.

Cool, remove from the parchment paper and cut into 12 long pieces. Julienne the pieces into mini-strips.

Ingredients/Micro Basil and Fennel Salad

1 cup micro basil

1/2 bulb fresh fennel

1 cup olive oil

1/2 cup balsamic vinegar

1/2 bunch chervil

1/2 cup tomato leather pieces

Method/Micro Basil and Fennel Salad

Shave fennel bulb as fine as possible. Toss the shavings with the olive oil and balsamic vinegar.

Just before serving, add chervil leaves, micro basil and tomato leather strips and toss.

Ingredients/Parmesan Crisp

1 cup shredded Parmesan cheese

Method/Parmesan Crisp

On a 1/2 sheet pan covered with parchment paper, spoon the Parmesan into 10 long strips to form Parmesan sticks. Bake the Parmesan at 350° for 10 minutes, or until it becomes light golden brown.

Remove from the oven and let cool.

Assembly

Place Tomato Confit at the bottom of each service cup or glass and top with Tomato Leather. Put a little salad on top, off to one side, and place a Parmesan Crisp on the side of the salad.

Cheese PRESENTATIONS

BLUE CHEESE ◆ BACON ◆ ONION
PEPATO CHEESE ◆ SPINACH ◆ BUTTERNUT SQUASH
PARMESAN ◆ BASIL ◆ ONION
MOZZARELLA ◆ OLIVES ◆ ONION

Stick

Spoon

Glass

Marinated Ciliengine
Mozzarella with
Pickled Onions and
Kalamata Olives

Mozzarella Roulade
with Basil Marinated
Onions and Truffle
Olive Oil Dust

Mozzarella Perlini with
Red Onion Salad and
Olive Vinaigrette

174

176

178

Marinated Ciliengine Mozzarella with Pickled Onions and Kalamata Olives

Ingredients/Marinated Ciliengine Mozzarella

40 ciliengine mozzarella (small fresh mozzarella balls)

1/2 bunch fresh basil, chopped

kosher salt

white pepper

1/4 tsp red pepper flakes

2 garlic cloves, chopped

40 kalamata olives, pitted (for assembly)

1/2 bunch fresh basil leaves, chopped (for assembly)

Method/Marinated Ciliengine Mozzarella

Combine the spices and toss the garlic in them, then let marinate for 3 hours in refrigerator.

Put the olives aside.

Ingredients/Pickled Onions

40 fresh pearl onions

1 cup balsamic vinegar

1 cup tomato juice

1/2 cup sugar

1/2 bunch basil, chopped

2 stalks rosemary leaves, chopped

2 garlic cloves, chopped

Method/Pickled Onions

Put all ingredients together in a saucepan. Bring to a simmer, then shut the heat off and allow to steep for 4 hours.

Remove from heat and place in refrigerator overnight.

Before service, remove the onions from the liquid and lightly dry, removing any excess liquid.

Ingredients/Tomato Gelée

1 cup tomato juice

2 1-oz packets of powdered gelatin

1/2 cup chicken stock

1/4 bunch fresh basil, chopped

Method/Tomato Gelée

Combine the chicken stock and gelatin, let gelatin dissolve.

Add the fresh basil to chicken stock. Add the tomato juice.

Pour mixture into 1/2-inch silicone molds

Chill until set, about 4 hours.

Assembly

For each skewer: Start with 1 olive, then 1 mozzarella ball, 1 cube of Tomato Gelée, 1 pearl onion and 1 more mozzarella ball.

Sprinkle chopped basil over skewers just before serving.

Chef Notes

Marinating all items ahead of time creates a stronger flavor profile.

The pearl onions can be done up to 2 days ahead of time. Be careful to simmer, not boil, or the onions will get too soft.

Variations

Give this hors d'oeuvre a "meatier" flavor by adding grilled cremini mushrooms. Make it more of a Mediterranean flavor profile by making a basil gelée instead of the tomato gelée and using Greek green olives.

Chef Notes
The packaged roll of mozzarella is flexible and very forgiving. The cheese picks up flavors well, so you can experiment with a variety of roasted vegetable and vinegars for different flavors.

Variations
Use portobello mushrooms instead of red peppers for a meatier dish.

CHEESE PRESENTATIONS

Mozzarella Roulade with Basil Marinated Onions and Truffle Olive Oil Dust

Ingredients/Mozzarella Roulade

1 Unwrap & Roll Mozzarella™ from BelGioioso

20 fresh basil leaves

2 red peppers

8 oz pepperoni

kosher salt

white pepper

olive oil

Method/Mozzarella Roulade

Brush the red peppers with olive oil, season with salt and pepper. Roast in a 350° oven for 30 minutes, or until skin starts to blister. Take the peppers out of the oven and put into a metal bowl covered with plastic; let cool. Once cooled, remove the skins and seeds and wash lightly in plain water. Cut off the top and bottom of the peppers and slit down one side so each opens into one long piece. Set aside.

Unroll the mozzarella sheets on a work surface.

Slice the pepperoni paper-thin and lay the slices on the sheets of mozzarella.

Lay basil leaves on top of the pepperoni.

Put the roasted red pepper on top of the basil.

Roll the mozzarella into a log, then wrap in plastic and twist the ends to create a vacuum.

Refrigerate roulade overnight.

Ingredients/Truffle Olive Oil Dust

1 cup truffle olive oil

2 cups maltodextrin

kosher salt

white pepper

Method/Truffle Olive Oil Dust

Place oil in a food processor, add the maltodextrin and process until dust forms. Season with salt and pepper.

Pass the dust through a China cap to remove lumps.

Set aside until service.

Ingredients/Basil Marinated Onions

10 red pearl onions

1 bunch fresh basil, chopped

1 cup olive oil

1/2 cup white balsamic vinegar

kosher salt

white pepper

1/4 tsp red pepper flakes

2 garlic cloves, chopped

Method/Basil Marinated Onions

Cut off the tops and bottoms of the pearl onions and peel them, then shave on a Japanese slicer and place in a mixing bowl. Add the rest of the ingredients. Marinate overnight in the refrigerator.

Assembly

Slice the roulade into 20 pieces. Put a piece in each spoon.

Drain the liquid from the marinating onions. Place a tsp of the onion mixture in the center of each piece of roulade.

Spoon 1/2 tsp Truffle Dust on top of the onions and roulade. Garnish with micro basil.

CHEESE PRESENTATIONS

Makes about 20 servings

Mozzarella Perlini with Red Onion Salad and Olive Vinaigrette

Ingredients/Mozzarella Perlini

6 oz mozzarella perlini (small balls of mozzarella)

1 cup sundried tomatoes

2 sprigs fresh rosemary leaves, chopped

5 garlic cloves, chopped

1 cup olive oil

kosher salt

white pepper

Method/Mozzarella Perlini

Sauté garlic and rosemary in 1/4 cup olive oil for about 2-3 minutes. Season with salt and pepper

Julienne the sundried tomatoes and place them in a blender. Add 3/4 cup olive oil and purée until the sundried tomatoes are fully broken down and a tomato oil forms.

Drain the perlini and toss with the sundried tomato oil and garlic mixture combined; refrigerate overnight.

Ingredients/Red Onion Salad

1 red onion

2 tsp red wine vinegar

1/2 cup celery leaves

1 cup snow pea shoots

4 tsp walnut oil

Method/Red Onion Salad

Shave the red onion paper thin and combine with the celery leaves and pea shoots. Just before service, toss with the red wine vinegar and walnut oil.

Ingredients/Olive Vinaigrette

1 cup kalamata olives, pitted

1 cup walnut oil

1 sprig fresh thyme

Method/Olive Vinaigrette

Remove the thyme leaves from the stem and put into a blender. Add the olives and oil and purée.

Let flavors blend overnight in refrigerator. Just before service, strain into a squeeze bottle.

Ingredients/Basil Crumb

1 cup panko breadcrumbs

1/2 bunch fresh basil leaves

1/4 cup olive oil

kosher salt

white pepper

Method/Basil Crumb

Process the basil and breadcrumbs in a food processor until blended. Slowly add the oil while processing. Season with salt and pepper.

Reserve for service in an airtight container

Assembly

Place a Tbsp of mozzarella into each service cup or glass. Spoon some onion salad on top of the mozzarella and drizzle Olive Vinaigrette on the salad. Finish with a sprinkling of Basil Crumbs.

Chef Notes
Be sparing with the olive vinaigrette; it has a very strong flavor.

Variations
You can use marinated artichokes or tomatoes in the salad, instead of the marinated onions, with a sundried tomato vinaigrette instead of the olive vinaigrette.

CHAPTER SIX

Dessert
CREATIONS

CHOCOLATE ◆ RASPBERRY ◆ PISTACHIO
CARAMEL ◆ APPLE ◆ BRANDY
PEANUT BUTTER ◆ CHOCOLATE ◆ HAZELNUT
BANANA ◆ VANILLA ◆ COFFEE

End the party with a delightful bite of something sweet—or create a whole event around an array of dessert hors d'oeuvre. The kinds of flavors and ingredients that go into dessert items are perfect on a skewer, in a spoon or in a mini-glass or cup.

As with most desserts, many of the key elements of these recipes can be changed easily to create something completely different—although there may be no good reason, ever, to substitute for chocolate.

Dessert CREATIONS

CHOCOLATE ◆ RASPBERRY ◆ PISTACHIO
CARAMEL ◆ APPLE ◆ BRANDY
PEANUT BUTTER ◆ CHOCOLATE ◆ HAZELNUT
BANANA ◆ VANILLA ◆ COFFEE

Chocolate Ganache
with Raspberry Gelée
and Pistachio
Marshmallow

Raspberry Mousse with
Chocolate Crumb and
Pistachio Anglaise
Spheres

Chocolate Raspberry
Cake with White
Chocolate Mousse and
Pistachio Brittle

184

186

188

Chef Notes

*Making marshmallows can be tricky.
Be sure to give the marshmallow enough time
to dry well or it will be difficult to work with.*

Variations

*It's easy to change this dessert hors
d'oeuvre by simply adding a flavor to the
marshmallow. Flavors such as green tea
extract, peanut butter or passionfruit can
be added to the marshmallow once the basic
mixture has been completed. Add a small
amout at a time to keep the marshmallow
mixture from becoming too loose,
which will keep the marshmallows
from firming up properly.*

Makes about 20 servings

Chocolate Ganache with Raspberry Gelée and Pistachio Marshmallow

Ingredients/Chocolate Ganache

8 oz dark chocolate, chopped into small pieces

3/4 cup heavy whipping cream

2 Tbsp unsalted butter

1 Tbsp cognac

Method/Chocolate Ganache

Place the chopped chocolate in a medium-sized stainless steel bowl. Set aside.

Heat the cream and butter in a medium saucepan over medium heat for about 12 minutes, until it just comes to a boil.

Immediately pour the boiling cream over the chocolate and let stand for 5 minutes. Whisk until smooth, then add the cognac. Pour chocolate into 2-inch-square rubber molds, filling to the top.

Ingredients/Raspberry Gelée

1 (1/4-oz) envelope unflavored gelatin

2 Tbsp cold water

16 oz raspberries, fresh or frozen

1/2 cup granulated sugar

Method/Raspberry Gelée

Bloom the gelatin in the cold water, then set aside.

Purée the raspberries in a blender. Strain through a fine-mesh strainer to take out the seeds.

Combine the purée and the sugar in a medium saucepan over 15 minutes heat and heat until it comes to a simmer, about 6 minutes, stirring often to make sure the sugar is dissolved.

Remove the purée and sugar from the heat and mix in the gelatin and water mixture. Mix in well, then strain the mixture through a fine-mesh strainer set over a clean mixing bowl. Once strained, allow to cool and then refrigerate until the gelée is set, about 1 hour.

Ingredients/Pistachio Marshmallows

1 cup cold water, divided

3 1/4-oz envelopes unflavored gelatin

2 cups granulated sugar

1 cup light corn syrup

1/4 tsp salt

2 tsp pure vanilla extract

1 cup pistachios, chopped

Method/Pistachio Marshmallow

Lightly butter or spray with a nonstick vegetable spray, the bottom of a 9x13-inch baking pan with 2-inch sides. Line the bottom of the pan with parchment paper. Then sift about 3 Tbsp of confectioners' (powdered or icing) sugar onto the bottom of the pan (this will help release the marshmallows from the paper).

Place 1/2 cup cold water into the bowl of an electric mixer fitted with a whisk attachment. Sprinkle the gelatin over the water and let stand until gelatin softens, about 15 minutes.

Put the sugar, corn syrup, salt and remaining 1/2 cup cold water in a heavy 2-quart saucepan. Stir over medium heat until sugar dissolves and the mixture comes to a boil, about 11 minutes. Cover the saucepan and let the mixture boil for about 3 minutes to allow any sugar crystals to dissolve from the sides of the saucepan. Remove the lid and attach a candy thermometer to the side of the pan. Increase the heat to high and boil, without stirring, until the syrup reaches 240°, about 10 minutes. Remove from heat.

With the mixer running at low speed, slowly pour the hot syrup into the gelatin mixture in a thin stream down the side of the bowl. Gradually increase the speed to high and beat until mixture has tripled in volume and is very thick and stiff, about 10 minutes (it will look like thick creme of marshmallow). Add vanilla extract and beat to combine, about 30 seconds longer.

Scrape the marshmallow mixture into the prepared pan and spread with a damp offset spatula or rubber spatula. The mixture is very sticky, so just smooth it as best you can. Sprinkle the chopped pistachios on top and lightly dust the top of the marshmallow with another 3 Tbsp confectioners' sugar. Let stand, uncovered, at room temperature until set, about 12 hours.

Assembly

Cut the ganache, gelée and marshmallow into 1-1/2-inch squares. Put on skewers in this order: marshmallow, gelée, marshmallow, ganache, marshmallow.

Ingredients/Chocolate Crumb

1 cup (2 sticks) butter or margarine, softened

1-3/4 cups all-purpose flour

1/2 cup granulated sugar

1/4 tsp salt

2 cups semi-sweet chocolate morsels

1 (14-oz) can sweetened condensed milk

1 tsp vanilla extract

Method/Chocolate Crumb

Beat the butter until creamy in a large mixing bowl. Beat in the flour, sugar and salt until crumbly.

With floured fingers, press 2 cups of the crumb mixture onto the bottom of a greased 9x13-inch baking pan. Reserve the remaining mixture.

Bake in a 350° oven for 10 to 12 minutes or until edges are golden brown.

Combine 1 cup of the chocolate morsels and the sweetened condensed milk in a small, heavy saucepan. Warm over low heat, stirring until smooth, about 6 minutes. Stir in the vanilla extract, then spread over the hot crust.

Stir the remaining morsels into the reserved crumb mixture; sprinkle over the chocolate filling. Bake at 350° for 25 to 30 minutes or until center is set. Cool in pan on wire rack.

Makes about 20 servings

Raspberry Mousse with Chocolate Crumb and Pistachio Anglaise Spheres

Ingredients/Pistachio Anglaise Spheres

1 cup (4 oz) shelled unsalted pistachios

2 cups milk

1/2 cup sugar

salt

8 large egg yolks

1/2 tsp pure almond extract

2 gm sodium alginate

150 ml pistachio anglaise

100 ml water

2 gm calcium chloride

500 ml water

Method/Pistachio Anglaise Spheres

Spread the shelled pistachios on a rimmed baking sheet and bake in a preheated 350° oven for 5 minutes, or until lightly toasted. Let cool completely, then rub the pistachios in a kitchen towel to remove the skins. Transfer the pistachios to a food processor and grind to a fine powder.

Put the milk and the ground pistachios in a medium saucepan and bring to a boil over medium heat, about 15-20 minutes. Cover, remove from the heat and let stand for 30 minutes.

Strain the pistachio milk through a fine sieve into another medium saucepan. Add the sugar and a pinch of salt. Whisk in the egg yolks and cook over low heat, whisking constantly, until the custard sauce is thick enough to coat the back of a spoon, about 8 minutes. Do not let the custard boil.

Strain the sauce through a fine sieve into a bowl. Stir in the almond extract and let cool, stirring often. Cover and refrigerate until ready to serve, approximately 20 minutes.

Combine the sodium alginate and the pistachio Anglaise together and puree. Strain mixture through a fine sieve, then either pull into a baster with a plunger on the end or put in a plastic squeeze bottle. Mix the calcium chloride and 100 ml water together in a bowl. Push or squeeze large drops of the pistachio Anglaise, one at a time, into the calcium chloride to make large spheres. Remove the spheres from the calcium chloride mixture after 20 seconds using a small strainer and drop into 500 ml cool water to remove any chloride flavor. Remove from water using a small strainer and hold in a plastic container for later use.

Ingredients/Raspberry Mousse

2 cups fresh or frozen raspberries

1 Tbsp unflavored gelatin

1 Tbsp lemon juice

4 cups chilled whipped cream

1/4 cup sugar

Method/Raspberry Mousse

In a saucepan, combine 1-1/2 cups raspberries, sugar and lemon juice. Heat and stir over medium heat until the raspberries become liquid, about 20 minutes. Stir in the gelatin. Remove from the heat and scrape into a large bowl. Let cool for 5 minutes.

Mix 1 cup of chilled whipped cream into the raspberry mixture until well combined. Fold in the remaining whipped cream. Place into a piping bag and set aside.

Assembly

Pipe some mousse into each spoon. Put an Anglaise sphere on top of the mousse and pipe a tiny bit of mousse on top of the sphere. Sprinkle Chocolate Crumb over the mousse.

Chef Notes
Anglaise spheres can be made up to one day ahead and held cold in an airtight container.

Variations
For a richer flavor, make dark chocolate spheres with a caramel mousse and mint chocolate crumbs.

CHEF ERIC LeVINE

Chef Notes

*If you are making the brittle the day before,
be sure to store in a cool dry place.*

*You can also use the brittle as a base, pipe the
mousse on top and sprinkle crumbs over it,
rather than putting it in a spoon or a cup.*

Variations

*It's easy to change this dessert completely by
making an amaretto cake with dark chocolate
mousse and caramelized hazelnut.*

Makes about 20 servings

Chocolate Raspberry Cake with White Chocolate Mousse and Pistachio Brittle

Ingredients/Chocolate Raspberry Cake

3/4 cup red raspberries

1–1/2 cups flour

6 Tbsp cocoa

2 tsp baking powder

1/2 tsp baking soda

1/2 cup butter

1–1/4 cups sugar

3 eggs, beaten

1 cup sour cream

2 tsp vanilla

Method/Chocolate Raspberry Cake

Purée the raspberries; set aside.

Combine the flour, cocoa, baking powder and baking soda in a mixing bowl; set aside.

In a separate bowl, cream the butter and sugar together. Add the beaten eggs and beat with whisk until light and fluffy, about 8-10 minutes. Add the sour cream and vanilla and beat again. Add the dry ingredients and mix until well blended.

Pour about 2/3 of the batter into a greased heart-shaped springform pan or a round 9- to 10-inch springform pan.

Add the puréed raspberries to the pan and swirl gently through the batter with a thin spatula or a knife. Add the remaining batter and gently level off the batter with a spatula.

Bake at 325° for 50 minutes to an hour, or until a toothpick inserted in the center of the cake comes out clean.

Place on a wire rack and allow the cake to cool in the pan. When the cake is cool, remove the sides of the pan

Ingredients/Pistachio Brittle

1 cup sugar

1/2 cup light corn syrup

1/8 tsp salt

1 tsp butter (no substitutes)

1/2 cup shelled pistachio nuts

1 tsp baking soda

1 tsp vanilla extract

Method/Pistachio Brittle

In a 2-qt microwave-safe bowl, combine sugar, corn syrup and salt. Microwave, uncovered, on high for 4 minutes. Stir. Microwave 3 minutes longer.

Stir in butter and pistachios.

Microwave mixture on high for 30–60 seconds or until mixture turns a light amber (it will be very hot).

Quickly stir in baking soda and vanilla until light and foamy.

Immediately pour onto a greased baking sheet and spread out. Refrigerate for 20 minutes or until firm, then break into small pieces. Store in an airtight container.

Ingredients/White Chocolate Mousse

1 cup white chocolate chips

1/4 cup water

2/3 cup sugar

1 cup whipping cream

1 tsp vanilla

Method/White Chocolate Mousse

Mix water and sugar in a saucepan and heat over medium heat until sugar is dissolved, 18-20 minutes.

Add chocolate chips and melt until smooth, about 20 minutes.

Set saucepan in cold water to cool mixture. Place in the refrigerator until thoroughly chilled, about 20-30 minutes, then whisk until smooth.

Beat the cream and vanilla until stiff peaks form. Fold the cream into the cold chocolate mixture.

Cover and reserve in refrigerator for later use.

Assembly

Spoon some chocolate cake into each service cup or glass. Pipe some mousse on the cake. Break off a piece of the brittle and stick it into the mousse.

Dessert CREATIONS

CHOCOLATE ◆ RASPBERRY ◆ PISTACHIO

CARAMEL ◆ APPLE ◆ BRANDY

PEANUT BUTTER ◆ CHOCOLATE ◆ HAZELNUT

BANANA ◆ VANILLA ◆ COFFEE

Stick

Spoon

Glass

Caramel Fudge with
Caramelized Apple and
Brandy Crumbs

Apple Mousse with
Brandy Doughnuts and
Cinnamon Caramel

Caramel Mousse with
Brandy Glaze and
Apple Tartan

192

194

196

Caramel, Apple, Brandy

Caramel Fudge with Caramelized Apple and Brandy Crumbs

Ingredients/Caramel Fudge

3 cups sugar

1 cup cream

1/4 cup butter

2 Tbsp white corn syrup

1/8 tsp salt

Method/Caramel Fudge

Lightly brown 1 cup of sugar in a heavy pan over medium heat, about 15-20 minutes. Slowly add the cream, remaining sugar, butter, syrup and salt.

Cook to soft ball stage or 235° on candy thermometer, about 20 minutes.

Remove from heat; beat with whisk until thick. Pour in buttered half hotel pan and refrigerate for later use.

Ingredients/Caramelized Apple

1 Granny Smith apple

1 cup sugar

1/2 cup water

Method/Caramelized Apple

Peel the apple. Using a large melon baller (22 mm), scoop the apple into consistent balls.

Combine the sugar and water in heavy-gauge pan over high heat and lightly brown, about 20 minutes. Add the apple balls and cook for about 5 minutes, until caramelized. Remove from heat once the apples have an overall golden color, then remove apples from caramel and reserve.

Ingredients/Brandy Crumbs

1 cup all-purpose flour

1/2 cup firmly packed brown sugar

1/2 tsp cinnamon

1/2 cup butter

2 tsp brandy

Method/Brandy Crumbs

Combine all ingredients in a mixing bowl and mix with spoon until it's a coarse crumb.

Set aside.

Assembly

Cut the fudge into 2-inch squares.

Skewer a piece of Caramelized Apple, then a piece of fudge.

Sprinkle Brandy Crumbs on all sides of the skewer before service.

Chef Notes

The fudge can be made up to a week in advance and stored in a cool dry space.

Dry the apple cores in a dehydrator or low-temperature oven to use as a garnish for the passing tray

Variations

Instead of apples, use pears and make a cinnamon pumpkin fudge for a great fall dessert.

Apple Mousse with Brandy Doughnuts and Cinnamon Caramel

Ingredients/Apple Mousse

3 medium-sized cooking apples or Granny Smith apples, peeled, quartered and cored

3-1/2 oz water

1/2 oz white sugar

1/4 tsp lemon juice

10 oz farmhouse cider
(with some pulp in it) or fresh cider

1-1/2 tsp powdered gelatin

1 cup whipping cream

Method/Apple Mousse

Place the apples in a saucepan over medium heat and add water, sugar and lemon juice. Simmer for 10 minutes until the apples are tender and just starting to break down. Purée in a food processor and push through a fine sieve.

In another saucepan, boil the cider for about 12 minutes, until reduced to about 5 Tbsp. Remove from heat and sprinkle the powdered gelatin over it. Stir until the gelatin is dissolved, then let cool for 5 minutes.

Whip the cream until it forms soft peaks and fold in the apple purée and cider. Place into a half hotel pan, smooth the surface and leave to set in the refrigerator for 2 hours.

Ingredients/Brandy Doughnuts

6 tsp or 2 packets of dry yeast

1/2 cup warm water

1 cup + 1 pinch sugar

7 cups all-purpose flour

2 cups boiling water

1/2 cup brandy

2 tsp vanilla

1/2 tsp grated nutmeg

zest of 1 lemon

2 qts frying oil

Method/Brandy Doughnuts

Mix the yeast with the warm water and a pinch of sugar and set aside until risen and foamy, about 5 minutes. Place the flour in a large bowl and create a well in the middle. Add the boiling water gradually and blend with a wooden spoon. Keep stirring until the dough begins to form a ball.

Continue beating as you gradually add the 1 cup sugar, brandy, vanilla, nutmeg, raisins and lemon rind. Blend in the yeast mixture and then let the batter rest for 15 to 20 minutes.

Heat the cooking oil in a deep pot. When the oil is hot enough (test by dropping in a small piece of the batter, which should sizzle, but not burn), drop in the batter by well-rounded 1/2 Tbsp measures. You will have to dip the measuring spoon in water between spoonfuls of batter to clean it off. You may also have to coax the batter off the spoon.

Do not overcrowd the frying pot. Ensure the doughnuts are turned so that all sides are golden. When browned, transfer with a slotted spoon to paper towels and let cool slightly

Ingredients/Cinnamon Caramel

2 cups sugar

1/2 cup water

1/4 cup hot water

6 Tbsp half-and-half

1/2 tsp kosher salt

1 (3-inch) cinnamon stick

Method/Cinnamon Caramel

Combine sugar and 1/2 cup water in a small, heavy saucepan over high heat; cook until sugar dissolves, stirring as needed to dissolve sugar evenly (about 2 minutes).

Cook another 8 minutes or until golden (do not stir).

Remove from heat; cool slightly. Carefully stir in 1/4 cup hot water, half-and-half and 1/2 tsp salt. Add the cinnamon stick and let cool to room temperature.

Pour the caramel into a 1-qt container. Cover and hold at room temperature until service

Assembly

Put some caramel into each serving spoon. Pipe mousse on top of the caramel, then swirl a little more caramel on the mousse. Finish with a doughnut..

Ingredients/Caramel Mousse

3/4 cup plus 3 Tbsp water

1 envelope unflavored gelatin

2-3/4 cups sugar

2 Tbsp light corn syrup

pinch salt

1-3/4 cups whipping cream at room temperature

2 oz unsalted butter

1-1/2 cups chilled whipping cream

Method/Caramel Mousse

Pour 3 Tbsp water into ramekin or custard cup. Sprinkle with gelatin; let soften while preparing caramel sauce.

Combine sugar, corn syrup and 3/4 cup water in heavy large saucepan. Stir over medium-low heat until sugar dissolves, about 15-20 minutes, frequently brushing down sides of pan with a wet pastry brush. Increase the heat and boil without stirring until the syrup turns deep golden brown, about 10 minutes, occasionally brushing down sides of pan with wet pastry brush and swirling pan. Remove from heat. Add 1-3/4 cups cream and the butter (caramel will bubble up vigorously). Return to low heat; stir until any bits of caramel dissolve, about 6 minutes.

Pour 1-1/2 cups caramel sauce into a glass measuring cup and set aside the pan of caramel sauce. The additional sauce can be used for garnish. Place the ramekin with gelatin mixture in a small skillet of simmering water. Stir until the gelatin dissolves and the mixture is clear, about 1 minute. Mix gelatin into measured 1-1/2 cups hot caramel; cool just to room temperature, stirring occasionally. Add salt and stir.

Beat the chilled whipping cream in a large bowl to medium-firm peaks (do not overbeat). Gradually pour the cooled caramel-gelatin mixture over the cream, folding constantly but gently. Chill the mousse at least 1 hour before use.

Makes about 20 servings

Caramel Mousse with Brandy Glaze and Apple Tartan

Ingredients/Apple Tartan

1 cup sugar

1/4 cup apple cider

1/2 lemon, juiced

1 vanilla bean, seeds scraped

1 stick butter, cut into pats

2 Granny Smith apples, peeled, cored and finely diced

Method/Apple Tartan

Place the apple, sugar, apple cider, lemon juice and vanilla bean seeds in a 10-inch nonstick ovenproof pan. Stir to combine.

Over high heat, bring the mixture to a boil, brushing down the sides of the pan occasionally with a pastry brush dipped in water. After 6–7 minutes, the mixture will begin to turn light brown.

Move the pan around gently to promote even cooking. Cook the mixture for another minute or so until the mixture becomes a deeper amber color. Remove from the heat and stir in the butter, 2 pats at a time.

Allow to cool at room temperature before placing in the refrigerator

Ingredients/Brandy Glaze

1 cup apple cider

1/4 cup water

1 cup sugar

2 Tbsp unsalted butter, cut into pieces

3/4 cup heavy cream

1 Tbsp pear brandy

pinch of salt

Method/Brandy Glaze

In a heavy medium saucepan, combine the water and sugar. Cook over medium-high heat, swirling the pan gently, until the sugar is dissolved and the syrup is clear; do not let the mixture boil. Increase heat to high, cover and boil the syrup without stirring for 2 minutes.

Uncover the saucepan and continue to boil the syrup until it begins to darken around the edges, about 20 minutes. Gently swirl the pan until the syrup turns a deep amber and just begins to smoke, about another 5 minutes.

Remove from heat and carefully beat the butter in with a wooden spoon until well blended. Stir in the cream until smooth. If the sauce becomes lumpy, return the pan to the stove and cook over low heat, stirring until smooth.

Remove from heat and stir in the apple cider, the pear brandy, and salt.

Ingredients/Pastry Discs

1 piece puff pastry, cut into 10 2-inch diameter circles

egg wash (1 egg beaten with 1 tsp water)

Method/Pastry Discs

Roll with dough docker or use a fork to punch small holes into dough to keep it from rising. Brush each circle with egg wash.

Bake 20 minutes in a 300° oven until golden brown, about 20 minutes.

Assembly

Place a pastry disc in the bottom of each cup. Spoon some apple mixture on top of the pastry, then pipe in some mousse. Top with the brandy glaze.

Chef Notes

Be careful not to assemble too early; the pastry disc will absorb the liquid from the apples and soften to an undesirable texture Don't assemble any more than 2 hours before service.

Variations

Another twist on this item would be to caramelize pineapples, pipe a kiwi coconut mousse and drizzle mango caramel sauce on top.

Dessert
CREATIONS

CHOCOLATE ◆ RASPBERRY ◆ PISTACHIO

CARAMEL ◆ APPLE ◆ BRANDY

PEANUT BUTTER ◆ CHOCOLATE ◆ HAZELNUT

BANANA ◆ VANILLA ◆ COFFEE

Stick

Spoon

Glass

Chocolate Cheesecake
and Peanut Butter
Cheesecake with
Toasted Hazelnuts

200

Peanut Butter
Panna Cotta with
Hazelnut Cream and
Hazelnut Dust

202

Peanut Butter Mousse
and Chocolate Mousse
with Hazelnut Sauce

204

Makes about 20 servings

Chocolate Cheesecake and Peanut Butter Cheesecake with Toasted Hazelnuts

Ingredients/Chocolate Cheesecake

3 lbs cream cheese

12 oz dark chocolate

24 oz sugar

2 oz cornstarch

12 oz sour cream

6 eggs

Method/Chocolate Cheesecake

Place the cream cheese in the bowl of an electric mixer and mix on low until creamy. Add all remaining items except chocolate, one at a time in the order listed, making sure to mix well and scrape the sides of the bowl after each addition.

Melt chocolate in a bowl over hot water bath until smooth. Once chocolate is melted, slowly add to cream cheese mix.

After all items are well mixed, a flavor element can be added to the cheesecake (for example, 500 g of mango purée, or any other type of purée, or pieces of items such as coconut).

Line a half-sheet pan with waxed paper and pour the mixture into the pan. Bake in a 275° oven until the mixture is set, about 30 minutes (it shouldn't be browned). Cool, then put the pan into the freezer. Once it is frozen hard, after about 3 hours, remove from the freezer and cut into 1-inch squares (or any other shape).

Ingredients/Peanut Butter Cheesecake

2 lbs cream cheese

1 lb peanut butter

24 oz sugar

2 oz cornstarch

12 oz sour cream

6 eggs

Method/Peanut Butter Cheesecake

Place the cream cheese in the bowl of an electric mixer and mix on low until creamy. Add remaining items one at a time in the order listed, making sure to mix well and scrape the sides of the bowl after each addition.

Line a half-sheet pan with waxed paper and pour the mixture into the pan. Bake in a 275° oven until the mixture is set, about 45 minutes (it shouldn't be browned). Cool, then put the pan into the freezer. Once it is frozen hard, after about 3 hours, remove from the freezer and scoop into 1-oz balls (or any other shape).

Ingredients/Toasted Hazelnuts

1 cup hazelnuts

Method/Toasted Hazelnuts

Toast nuts on a sheet pan in a 325° oven until golden brown, about 15 minutes. Remove from oven and cool, then finely chop nuts and reserve.

Assembly

Put 1 piece of each cheesecake flavor on a skewer. Roll the skewers in chopped hazelnuts. Top with a dab of peanut butter if you like.

Chef Notes
You can make the cheesecake squares up to two weeks in advance and freeze. When ready to use, thaw for about 20 minutes.

Variations
It's easy to change the cheesecake flavors and give this dish a completely new personality. For example: Lemon Mint Cheesecake and Raspberry Cheesecake squares can be dipped in egg white, then sprinkled with lemon zest and chopped mint.

Makes about 20 servings

Peanut Butter Panna Cotta with Hazelnut Cream and Hazelnut Dust

Ingredients/Peanut Butter Panna Cotta

2 cups heavy cream

1/2 cup sugar

1 vanilla bean

2 sheets of gelatin

6 Tbsp peanut butter

Method/Peanut Butter Panna Cotta

Bring 1/2 cup cream, sugar and vanilla bean to a boil. Fold in peanut butter. Remove from heat and cool to room temperature.

Soak the gelatin in 4 cups of cold water until soft, about 3–4 minutes. Drain through a small sieve and add to the hot cream mixture.

With a paring knife, open the vanilla bean and scrape the seeds into the cream mixture. Then strain the mixture through a sieve and let cool.

Whip 1-1/2 cups of heavy cream until stiff, then fold into the cooled and strained cream mixture.

Spoon 1 tsp of the panna cotta into each serving spoon and place in the refrigerator for at least 2 hours or overnight.

Ingredients/Hazelnut Dust

2 tsp hazelnut oil

6 tsp maltodextrin

Method/Hazelnut Dust

Put hazelnut oil into a food processor. Slowly add the maltodextrin to the oil until it's fully incorporated and a fine dust forms. This will take about 4 minutes.

Pass mixture through a China cap to remove any lumps. Reserve at room temperature until service.

Ingredients/Hazelnut Whipped Cream

1 cup heavy cream

1/2 cup fine chopped hazelnuts

Method/Hazelnut Whipped Cream

Combine ingredients in the bowl of a stand mixer and whip at high speed until stiff peaks form.

Assembly

Remove the spoons filled with Peanut Butter Panna Cotta from the refrigerator. Pipe Hazelnut Whipped Cream on top. Sprinkle Hazelnut Dust on top to finish, then add two chocolate sticks (can be purchased or made) to garnish.

Chef Notes

When making the dust, be sure to pass the dust through a fine strainer to get out any larger pieces. You can make the dust up to three days in advance and then keep it in a plastic container in cool dry place.

Variations

The dish can take on a light, spring flavor profile if you make a raspberry-mint panna cotta with lime dust and strawberry whipped cream, garnished with white chocolate sticks.

Chef Notes
Be careful to cook the sugar out when making the hazelnut sauce or you will have a grainy sauce. If this occurs, add a little more water and continue to cook out sugar.

Variations
You can change the flavors of any element of this dish. Make strawberry and vanilla mint mousses with pistachios, or caramel and fig mousses with almonds.

Peanut Butter Mousse and Chocolate Mousse with Hazelnut Sauce

Makes about 20 servings

Ingredients/Peanut Butter Mousse

3 oz cream cheese

1 cup powdered sugar

1/4 cup milk

3/4 cup peanut butter

2 cups heavy cream

1 Tbsp vanilla

Method/Peanut Butter Mousse

Cream the cream cheese with powdered sugar in the bowl of a stand mixer with balloon whisk attachment. Add the milk and peanut butter. In a separate mixing bowl, whip the cream and vanilla. Once they are incorporated, fold into the peanut butter mixture.

Ingredients/Chocolate Mousse

4-1/2 oz bittersweet chocolate, finely chopped

2 Tbsp (1 oz) unsalted butter, diced

2 Tbsp espresso or very strong coffee

1 cup chilled heavy cream

3 large eggs, separated

1 Tbsp sugar

Method/Chocolate Mousse

Whip the cream to soft peaks, then refrigerate.

Combine the chocolate, butter, and espresso in the top of a double boiler over hot, but not simmering, water, stirring frequently until smooth. Remove from the heat and let cool until the chocolate is just slightly warmer than body temperature. To test, dab some chocolate on your bottom lip. It should feel warm. If it is too cool, the mixture will seize when the other ingredients are added.

Once the melted chocolate has cooled slightly, whip the egg whites in a medium bowl until they are foamy and beginning to hold a shape. Sprinkle in the sugar and beat until soft peaks form.

When the chocolate has reached the proper temperature, stir in the yolks. Gently stir in about one-third of the whipped cream. Fold in half the whites just until incorporated, then fold in the remaining whites, and finally the remaining whipped cream.

Refrigerate for at least 8 hours.

Ingredients/Hazelnut Sauce

1/2 cup and 1 Tbsp hazelnuts

3/4 cup sugar

3 Tbsp butter or margarine, cut into chunks

1/2 cup whipping cream

1/4 cup hazelnut-flavor liqueur

Method/Hazelnut Sauce

Put hazelnuts in an 8- or 9-inch pan. Bake in a 350° oven until the nuts are golden under skins, about 15 to 20 minutes. Pour onto a clean towel and, when cool enough to touch, rub nuts with fabric to loosen skins. Lift nuts from towel; discard skins. Coarsely chop nuts.

In a 10- to 12-inch nonstick frying pan over high heat, combine sugar and butter. Shake pan frequently to mix until sugar and butter are melted and amber colored, about 5 minutes; watch carefully.

Off the heat, add whipping cream (the mixture will foam); stir until caramel is smoothly mixed with cream. Stir in chopped nuts and liqueur.

Return sauce to medium heat and stir until boiling vigorously, about 6 minutes. The sauce can be served hot or cold.

Chop the remainder of hazelnuts and hold for service.

Assembly

Pipe Peanut Butter Mousse and Chocolate Mousse side by side in service glasses or cups. Put Hazelnut Sauce into pipettes and stick one into each glass. Finish with chopped hazelnuts.

Dessert
CREATIONS

CHOCOLATE ◆ RASPBERRY ◆ PISTACHIO
CARAMEL ◆ APPLE ◆ BRANDY
PEANUT BUTTER ◆ CHOCOLATE ◆ HAZELNUT
BANANA ◆ VANILLA ◆ COFFEE

Caramelized Banana with
Vanilla Bean Cookie and
Coffee Cream Dip

Vanilla Bean Custard
with Coffee Caramel,
Banana Mousse and
Banana Crisps

Coffee Mousse with
Banana Paper and
Coffee Crumb

208

210

212

Chef Notes
Keep the cookies at room temperature;
they will soften in the refrigerator.

A skewer that's too big will crack the cookies.

Variations
You can give this a fall twist by making
cinnamon cookies, caramel dip and
caramelized apples.

Makes about 20 servings

Caramelized Banana with Vanilla Bean Cookie and Coffee Cream Dip

Ingredients/Caramelized Banana

2 tsp unsalted butter

1 banana, halved, then each half sliced lengthwise

2 tsp packed brown sugar

2 Tbsp rum (preferably dark)

2 tsp water

1/8 tsp freshly grated nutmeg

1/8 tsp cinnamon

salt

Method/Caramelized Banana

Melt butter in a heavy 10-inch skillet over moderately high heat until foam subsides, about 2 minutes, then sauté banana, cut sides down, while shaking skillet, about 1 minute.

Remove skillet from heat and sprinkle brown sugar around banana, then pour rum around banana.

Return skillet to heat and continue to sauté, shaking skillet occasionally, until sugar begins to melt, about 30 seconds.

Add water, nutmeg, cinnamon and a pinch of salt and cook over moderate heat, shaking skillet occasionally, until sauce is slightly thickened, 1–2 minutes.

Ingredients/Vanilla Bean Cookie

6 Tbsp unsalted butter, softened

2 Tbsp cold vegetable shortening

1 cup sugar

2 vanilla beans

1 large egg

1 tsp vanilla extract

1-1/4 cups all-purpose flour

1 tsp baking powder

1/2 tsp salt

Method/Vanilla Bean Cookie

With an electric mixer, beat together the butter, shortening and 3/4 cup sugar until light and fluffy.

Halve the vanilla beans lengthwise. Scrape the seeds into the butter mixture and beat in egg and vanilla extract until combined well. Sift flour, baking powder and salt into the mixture and beat until just combined.

On a large sheet of wax paper, form the dough into a 10x2-inch log and roll up in wax paper. Chill dough until firm, at least 4 hours. Dough keeps up to 3 days wrapped in wax paper and foil.

Spread the remaining 1/4 cup sugar on a platter. Take the dough out of the wax paper and roll the log in the sugar, then cut the log into ¼-inch slices. Dip the cut sides of the slices in the remaining sugar on the platter.

Arrange the cookies 1/2 inch apart on ungreased baking sheets and bake in batches at 375° in middle of oven 10–12 minutes or until edges are light gold.

With a metal spatula, transfer the cookies to a rack to cool. Cookies may be made two days ahead of use.

Ingredients/Coffee Cream Dip

1 tsp instant coffee granules

1 tsp hot water

1 cup chilled whipping cream

2 Tbsp powdered sugar

Method/Coffee Cream Dip

Dissolve instant coffee in 1 tsp hot water in small bowl.

Whip cream and sugar until medium-soft peaks form.

Add the coffee mixture to the cream and continue beating until stiff peaks form.

Reserve in refrigerator until service

Assembly

For each skewer, use two cookies. Spoon a dollop of coffee cream on each cookie, then put a piece of Caramelized Banana on one of the cookies. Top the banana with the other cookie, then skewer.

Chef Notes
You can find high-quality banana chips at specialty food stores, if you want to save time making the recipe.

Variations
For a holiday winter feel change the custard flavor to eggnog, the mousse to cinnamon and the banana chips to an almond crisp.

Makes about 20 servings

Vanilla Bean Custard with Coffee Carmel, Banana Mousse and Banana Crisps

Ingredients/Vanilla Bean Custard

2-1/2 cups milk

3/4 cup sugar

1/3 cup all-purpose flour

2 egg yolks

2 tsp vanilla bean paste (or 2 tsp vanilla extract)

Method/Vanilla Bean Custard

Whisk the milk, sugar, flour and egg yolks together in a heavy 3-qt saucepan.

Cook over medium-heat, whisking constantly, 10–12 minutes or until thickened.

Remove from heat; stir in vanilla bean paste. Cover and chill 3 hours.

Ingredients/Coffee Caramel

2-1/2 tsp instant espresso powder

3 Tbsp hot water

2/3 cup plus 1/2 cup sugar

1/4 lb butter

Method/Coffee Caramel

Stir espresso powder and hot water together until powder is dissolved.

Cook 1/2 cup sugar with a pinch of salt in a heavy saucepan over moderate heat, undisturbed, until it begins to melt. Continue to cook, stirring occasionally with a fork, until the sugar is melted into a deep golden caramel, about 15 minutes.

Remove the caramel from the heat and whisk in the espresso (the mixture will steam and bubble vigorously). Slowly add pieces of butter and whisk together until caramel is room temperature.

Ingredients/Banana Mousse

1/4 cup sugar

1/3 cup water

4 ripe bananas, peeled and sliced

1/4 tsp cinnamon

3 egg whites, beaten stiff

1 cup heavy cream, whipped

Method/Banana Mousse

Cook sugar and water together over medium heat for about 1 minute. Add the bananas and cinnamon and cook 3 minutes over medium-high heat.

Transfer the banana mixture to a food processor and purée.

Chill for at least 45 minutes.

After the banana purée is chilled, put it in a mixing bowl and fold in the beaten egg whites until they are well incorporated.

Fold the banana-egg white mixture into the whipped cream in a large bowl until well incorporated.

Ingredients/Banana Crisps

1 banana, peeled

1/4 tsp turmeric powder

oil for deep frying

salt

Method/Banana Crisps

Put the banana in salted ice water (about 1 qt water with 1/2 tsp salt). Remove from water to slice, then put back into water and add turmeric to the bowl. Keep the bananas in the water for 10 minutes, then drain completely and put on a kitchen cloth to remove the moisture.

Heat the oil until it starts fuming, Make a paste of 1/2 tsp water and 1/4 tsp salt and add it to the oil. This will make the slices fry crispier. Deep-fry the banana slices until they're crisp, about 5 minutes. Fry only a few slices at a time; don't crowd the fryer.

Drain the chips on an absorbent paper.

Cool and store in an airtight container for up to 5 days.

Assembly

Spoon a little custard into each spoon. Pipe Banana Mousse on top, drizzle on a little caramel. Stick banana chips into the mousse.

Makes about 20 servings

Coffee Mousse with Banana Paper and Coffee Crumb

Ingredients/Coffee Mousse

3 Tbsp strong coffee

2 Tbsp brandy

4 oz semisweet chocolate, chopped

2 Tbsp sugar

1 cup whipping cream

2 tsps sugar

1/4 tsp vanilla extract

Method/Coffee Mousse

Combine the coffee, brandy and chocolate in the top of a double boiler.

Heat over hot, not boiling, water until chocolate is melted. Stir in 2 Tbsp of the sugar and stir until the mixture is smooth and glossy, about 20 minutes.

Cool completely.

In a small, chilled bowl, beat the cream until thick. Beat in the remaining sugar and vanilla extract.

Fold in the cooled chocolate mixture. Refrigerate until firm, at least 3 hours.

Ingredients/Banana Paper

1 ripe banana

1 silicone mat

Method/Banana Paper

Purée the banana and spread evenly onto the silicone mat.

Bake at 325° for 10 minutes, until the banana spread is light brown.

Ingredients/Coffee Crumb

1/2 cup brown sugar

1/4 cup sifted all-purpose flour (sift before measuring)

1/4 cup butter, room temperature

1 tsp cinnamon

Method/Coffee Crumb

In small mixing bowl, combine topping ingredients. Blend with fork until crumbly. Set aside.

Assembly

Spoon 1 tsp of the crumb in the bottom of each cup or glass. Pipe mousse on top of the crumb until the cup is half filled. Put another 1 tsp of the crumb on top of the mousse, then pipe on more mousse and sprinkle on a little more crumb.

Put a 2x2-inch piece of banana paper into the mousse.

Chef Notes
When baking the "paper," be sure that you spread the mixture evenly on the mat so it will dry properly.

Variations
This can have a light, summer flavor profile with a key lime mousse, passionfruit crumbs and strawberry mint paper.

MOLECULAR GASTRONOMY

Equipment

*Some of the ingredients and kitchen tools may not be in your kitchen right now.
Here are descriptions of a few and how they are used.*

◆ **Calcium chloride** *is a salt traditionally used in cheese making. It's used with sodium alginate to "set" spheres of food that gel on the outside and are liquid in the center.*

◆ **Dehydrators** *remove moisture from food. Although often used to reduce spoiling, in these recipes, dehydrating foods is a way to change them in interesting ways.*

◆ **Foamers** *are used with natural flavors (such as fruit juices, infusions of aromatic herbs, etc) then mixed with a neutrally-flavored gelling or stabilizing agent like agar or lecithin, then whipped extruded through a whipped cream canister equipped with N2O cartridges. Foamers can be found at chefrubber.com.*

◆ **Japanese slicers** *have multiple blades for different slicing and cutting, yet are lightweight and easy to use and store. The Benriner Japanese Mandoline Slicer is the one that I have found to be the best value. It can be found at many Asian markets or at supply stores.*

◆ **Lecithin** *is an emulsifier and antioxidant. It can be used also as agent for de-molding very light pastries. Found through chefrubber.com.*

◆ **Maltodextrin** *is used to create oil-based "powders." It's made from a special tapioca. It can be purchased at chefrubber.com.*

◆ **Misting bottles** *let you spray a fine mist on food. The 15-ml bottles are available from Kosmetech in boxes of 200. When using individual misting bottles, be sure that the liquid being misted is strained until all impurities that might clog the mister are gone.*

◆ **Pearl droppers** *use a syringe and a dropper head that will make 96 "pearls" at a time.*

◆ **Silicone molds** *allow you to form cold or baked items. They are easy to clean and machine proof. After using the molds, simply soak or rinse them with hot water. If still dirty, use a soft sponge and some mild soap. Silicone molds come in various sizes and shapes and can be used at temperatures from -76° to 450°. They are available at chefrubber.com and in many kitchen supply stores and online.*

◆ **Sodium alginate** *is made from brown seaweed and is used to gel foods without heat. It has no flavor. In molecular gastronomy, sodium alginate is used with calcium chloride to make "caviar" and spheres. It's available at chefrubber.com.*

◆ **Transglutaminase** *improves the texture of emulsified meat products, such as sausages and hot dogs and is used to bind different meat parts together. It also makes milk products creamier and noodles firmer.*

CATERING *Resources*

Tabletop display, risers and platters
TableCraft Products Company
www.tablecraft.com

All-natural handcrafted cheeses
BelGioioso Cheese, Inc.
www.belgioioso.com

Plastic mini-servingware
EMI Yoshi, Inc.
www.emiyoshi.com

Natural bamboo skewers and party picks
Pick On Us, Inc
www.pickonus.com

Specialty food products and prep items
Chef Rubber
www.chefrubber.com

stick it
SPOON IT
PUT IT IN A GLASS

By CHEF ERIC LeVINE